Aristotle
POETICS

The Focus Philosophical Library
Series Editor • Albert Keith Whitaker

Aristotle
POETICS

**Translated, with
Introduction and Notes**

Joe Sachs
St. John's College, Annapolis

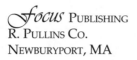 Publishing
R. Pullins Co.
Newburyport, MA

CONTENTS

Introduction

Experiencing and Thinking

There are a great many English translations of Aristotle's *Poetics*, and there is a wealth of commentary on it. The translations vary in accuracy, and the commentary varies in quality, but many of the former are serviceable and much of the latter is instructive. I venture to add to this already considerable accumulation of material for two reasons. The first is that no translation or discussion I have seen handles all the disputed points of interpretation as I would; the second is that the whole topic is so much fun. Some of the most exhilarating things an educated person can think about come tumbling out of Aristotle's inquiry into the questions of what a tragedy is, what it does, and how it does it. In the *Poetics* a human achievement of rare power and a thinker of rare depth met, and the world has never stopped talking about their encounter. Much of this talk has been critical, to the point of denying that Aristotle had any business daring to speak of something so foreign to his own specialties. But since his only specialty was thinking hard about anything that matters to a human being, such a critic has to be claiming that tragedy is incomprehensible by thinking, or that the experience of it is destroyed or diminished when it is subjected to thought.

Such a position is certainly a respectable one, but it loses some of its plausibility when one notices that so many people who clearly love tragedies choose to enter into passionate discussion with Aristotle, and with one another, about them. It is not in the nature of human beings to let things that interest us go unthought about. "What is it?" and "Why?" are not just modes of speaking and thinking; they are living ways of standing in and toward the world. In the face of our most powerful experiences, those questions may not get fully answered, but it is intolerable for them to go entirely unanswered either, and impossible for them to go unasked. For good or ill, to be greatly and noticeably affected by anything, and not to seek the cause, is no part of life as we live it. If that were not so, if we refrained from all reflection, important things could happen to us without becoming part of our experience at all. Life would pass through us without being lived by us.

1

This difference between what merely happens and what forms human experience is not only Aristotle's reason for striving to understand tragedy, it is at the heart of his understanding of tragedy. Just as we must make our own contribution to the things that happen to us to take them into our experience, we must make the decisive contribution to the things we do to lift them to the level of action. When Aristotle says that a tragedy sets before us an action that is serious and complete (1449b 24-25), he points us to the conditions of responsible human action that he discusses in the *Nicomachean Ethics*, in Chapters 2-5 of Book III. Action (*praxis*) is marked out there as dependent upon choice, and aimed at an end. It is for that reason that an action can have a completeness, despite the fact that the consequences of our deeds never end, and the totality of their causes could never be traced. The poet who shapes a work of art to disclose the unity of an action, as Homer shaped both the *Iliad* and the *Odyssey* (1451a 12-30), has an eye for the same aspects of life that Aristotle looks to in his thinking about ethics. It is not surprising, then, that we talk about the people in a tragedy as seriously as about the people we know, or that a vast number of the examples of actions that Aristotle gives throughout his study of ethics come from tragedies. Nor is it surprising if, to do justice to the whole of our experience, we find contributions from both poets and philosophers appropriate and welcome.

Imitation

Some of the resistance to Aristotle's discussion of poetry stems from his characterization of that activity as imitation (*mimêsis*), as though the poets' work is thereby tainted as something fake, like imitation leather. This sort of resistance often links Aristotle with Plato, who is thought to have treated poets with disrespect. On that issue, it may be sufficient for us to notice that in Plato's *Sophist*, imitative art is said to be capable of disclosing the true proportions of things (235 C-E). Such imitations would be of no great use if we could simply read those proportions off the originals of which they are copies. But Socrates, in Xenophon's *Memorabilia* (III, x, 1-8), points to their true use, when he asks about the fact that paintings and sculptures can be imitations (*mimêta*) not only of the look of a face or a body but also of the character and acts of a soul. I can attest that a certain lump of broken stone on display at Olympia in the Greek Peloponnese can be recognized not only as a standing man and as Apollo, but as radiating a calm dignity that overpowers the violent passions of the figures on his two sides. No one would ever confuse the interior life visible there with that in another block of graven stone in a Roman church, that is recognizably a seated man, and Moses, and angry, and controlling his anger.

Action, in the full sense described in the previous section, may be one of the most important things we could ever turn our attention to, and anything that helps us see it as it is would be a high achievement. But the worth of poetry is even greater if action can become visible nowhere but in an image. An action is stretched out in time, so that even in life, we can comprehend it nowhere but in the imagination. And its origin, in the act of choice, is interior, and never available to us in another person except by an act of interpretation. Even our own choices are not always recognized when they are made, but only evident to us retrospectively. And the ends for which we and others act, by which the outcomes of our deeds must be measured, are present to us only as possibilities foreseen in imagination. In the *Nicomachean Ethics*, Aristotle says that an action (*prakton*) is known only by sense perception (1142a 25-27), and then immediately qualifies this by saying that this is not the perception of any or all of the five external senses, but the same sort by which we perceive that a mathematical figure can be divided into no figures simpler than triangles. Try it. You might begin by drawing pictures and looking at them, but you will not come to a conclusion until you turn to the imagination.

To be an image of an action, what we see and hear on a stage must display the same interior depth that an action itself does. It is not enough that the figures before us be recognizable as Oedipus, Jocasta, and Tiresias, and go through motions, though that is the material with which the poet's activity works. From within that lowest level emerges the image that matters, of the invisible motions of a soul, as choices are made for reasons and consequences are faced. If the image on that higher level is capable of disclosing the true proportions of things to us, as the ranking of images in Plato's *Sophist* suggests, those proportions will have to do with the worth of choices, the respect due to the ends at which they aim, and the dignity of people who adhere to such choices for the sake of such ends. The imitations the poets offer us may be on a higher level than any originals we have managed to discern on our own.

Stories

Just as the imitation of an action reflects action itself in its dimension of depth, so too does it reflect the coherence of an action in its temporal extent (*megethos*), as beginning with a choice and seeking an end. Hence the beginning, middle, and end of a tragedy (1450b 21-34) are not its first, intermediate, and last episodes, but the inherent connections that constitute a well-made story (*muthos*). Most translations of the *Poetics* prefer to call this the "plot" of the tragedy, in part to distinguish the particular constructions put together by the various poets from the old stories out of which they take their material. But this makes a distinction of lesser importance overshadow a much more important point. Story-telling and our responses to it belong to a fundamental human experience that the tragic poets worked with just as much as they worked with known legends. The word "plot" may suggest a skeletal framework of events[1] onto which a poet can impose an illusion of life, but stories are genuine wholes that already have a life of their own; this is precisely what Aristotle means when he says that the story is like the soul of the tragedy (1450a 38-39).

An analogy to the role stories play in all fiction may be seen in the role melodies play in music. Victor Zuckerkandl begins his book *The Sense of Music* with the observation that we all know spontaneously when we have heard a melody that is not complete. The language of melody belongs to a human heritage that does not need to be taught or learned. Composers can work with or against this inherent grammar of melody in countless ways, but tones themselves are always active elements in any composition. In a melody, one tone feels central, and the rest are heard as pulling toward or away from it, establishing relations of tension and resolution. Likewise, in a story one or more characters become central in such a way that we anticipate events. Things that happen in a story are not neutral members of a series but arrive as things hoped for or feared, which, when they have happened, are met with feelings of satisfaction or regret.

Some people disdain stories as belonging to a shallow kind of literary sensibility, but the shallowness of such critics is greater. They are like people who, having seen that mere life is not enough for a human being, decide to give up breathing. The story is the soul of a tragedy not in the sense that it is the most important thing to be grasped about it, but in the sense that it is what breathes life into all the tragedy's parts, making them parts in the first place by giving them the internal references to one another that permits there to be a whole. Aristotle speaks of the parts of a tragedy sometimes in the sense of its qualitatively different forms of dramatic elements (Chap. 6), sometimes in the sense of its quantitative divisions into sections or scenes (Chap. 12), but it is only their coherence in a story that allows them all to be not just put together in a *sunthesis* but organized as a *sustasis*. Stories can be trivial as well as serious, manipulative as well as honest, but it is through the story that the poet makes his connection with the spectator; Aristotle not only calls the story the soul of the tragedy, he calls it the greatest of the means by which the poet draws our souls (1450a 33-34).

---

1   When Aristotle speaks of such a framework in Ch. 17, he calls it a *logos*.

Fear and Pity

The response of one who is drawn into the experience of a tragedy, according to Aristotle, is first of all to feel fear and pity (1449b 27). Some commentators think he meant these only as examples of a larger variety of emotional responses, and in the passage just cited he does subsequently refer to "feelings of that sort." Some other commentators think he meant just those two, but was arbitrarily restrictive in doing so. I believe that by "feelings of that sort" he meant just fear and pity, the first of which is a range of feelings extending from mild apprehension to terror, and the second of which covers a span from distant sympathy to empathetic misery; I believe too that he was characteristically perceptive in singling out just these two kinds of response. A little reflection on what is involved in following a story will begin to make clear what is peculiarly appropriate about them.

A story is not a series of events isolated like data points, but an unfolding motion that is continuous and one (1452a 15), no matter how much it may change or even reverse its direction. Aristotle says that the story in a tragedy must be complex, in the sense of containing some change of direction, but simple in the sense that what unfolds is all related to a single central character (1453a 12-13). It is by relation to the happiness or misery of that one character that the story comes to have a direction. If we are drawn toward that character rather than repulsed by him or her, our absorption in the story will dispose us to anticipate unfolding events with hope or fear, and to experience what comes to pass with gladness or regret. Other responses will always be involved, but these are the ones that must be present if we are experiencing a story at all. To say that a tragedy evokes fear and pity amounts to saying that, in the course of the action it imitates, some sort of harm gradually threatens and eventually overtakes the person whose action it portrays.

In his *Rhetoric*, Aristotle discusses in some detail the feelings a public speaker needs to understand. Since a deliberative assembly may be persuaded to act on the grounds that some threat is worthy of fear, and a jury may be persuaded to excuse some offense for the sake of pity, these two feelings are among them. In Bk. II, Chapter 5 of that work, Aristotle defines fear as "a certain pain or distress from the imagining of an impending evil of a destructive or painful sort," and concludes a description of its various causes by saying: "to put it simply, what is feared is whatever is pitied when it happens or is about to happen to others." In Chapter 8 of the same book he defines pity as "a certain pain at an evil of a destructive or painful sort that appears to happen to someone who doesn't deserve it," and concludes, "here too, in general, one needs to grasp that whatever things people fear for themselves they pity when they happen to others." The two kinds of response differ by referring to the future or the present, and to ourselves or to others. In our experience of a story, though, an anticipated future can come to be present, and our imaginations seem able to erase the boundary between ourselves and another. Pity by its nature always takes some share in the pain of another; our responsiveness to stories allows us to take on the pain of anticipated harm, at least for someone like ourselves (1453a 6); and the imitation of the wholeness of an action pairs these two kinds of shared pain in one experience.

To see better the effect of this pairing, it is instructive to think about what might happen if a story evoked fear without pity, or pity without fear. This turns out to be easy to do, since the first possibility is exactly what a horror story seems to be, and the second is what we call a tear-jerker. If my experience is typical, the intensity of fear aroused by Alfred Hitchcock's movie *Psycho* is unmatched by that of any tragedy, and in the ending of *City Lights*, Charlie Chaplin aimed at wringing every drop of pity out of a spectator's heart. Both directors were skilled at manipulating our emotions, and found vast audiences eager to submit to the process. If the effect of a tragedy depended simply on the height and depth of a roller-coaster of emotion, any horror/tear-jerker double feature could improve on any tragedy. If this seems impossible, even in the case of the best imaginable pair of semi-tragedies, that may be because the de-linking of fear and pity distances us from their sources. Even if fear gets into us more strongly in response to a horror story than in response to a tragedy, the thing feared seems to be external to both ourselves and the character or characters it threatens; the whole effect of a horror story seems to be the attachment of fear to some external image that we can walk away from at the end.[2] Similarly, the tears that the tear-jerker produces seem to have nothing to do with ourselves, but only to concern a make-believe world that we leave as easily and thoroughly as we enter it.

What is missing from these stories that single out fear or pity separately is the wholeness of an action, in which the fear felt through the middle and the pity felt at the end both stem from an original choice made by the character on whose behalf we are afraid and in whose suffering we share. The frightening things cannot merely be malicious enemies or an indifferent world, and what is pitiful cannot merely be that an undeserving person fell victim to hostile external forces, if the one who suffers harm bears direct responsibility for bringing it about. The central figure in a tragedy makes the choice that makes him vulnerable to the frightening things that destroy him. What we fear and what we pity are not neatly separated, allowing us to side with the undeserving

---

2   Aristotle says that the use of visual effects of a grotesque or monster-like (*teratôdes*) sort does not even produce fear, or have anything in common with tragedy (1453b 8-10).

victim and reject a malignant or unfeeling enemy. In taking the side of the victim for whom our fear and pity are aroused, we are compelled by a tragedy to accept from the start the choice that is his undoing.

The linking of fear and pity in a tragedy brings the source of harm within the image of the undeserving victim of it. And one more step shows us that this does not make the tragic figure some sort of bizarre aberration. We have seen that our very feelings of pity and fear include the sense of being for someone like ourselves, so we find ourselves too within the tragic figure's image. In the *Nicomachean Ethics*, Aristotle equates pity with the fellow-feeling (*sun-gnomê*) involved in forgiveness (1111a 1-2), and says that such a feeling is a recognition of human nature (1110a 25). The logic of our discussion has led us from the nature of action, through the union of destroyer and destroyed, to an image of human nature—that is, from human nature to human nature.

A Fatal Flaw

How can the tragic figure be both a pitiable victim and the responsible source of his own ruin? Most people would answer: by having a tragic flaw. There is something of a cottage industry that produces term papers for literature classes by hunting up tragic flaws. Among those who take this approach to tragedy, there are some who would contend that the moral of any tragedy is, if you have a flaw, you will be destroyed. Among those who see that the shallowness of this view makes a travesty of any tragedy, there are some who are convinced that Aristotle is the source of the shallowness. There are three problems with that conclusion. (a) Aristotle never said that the tragic figure has a flaw. (b) Aristotle did say what it is that causes the tragic figure's downfall, and it is something other than a flaw. (c) Aristotle's explanation of why only certain kinds of stories suit tragedies makes it plain that those in which a flawed character suffers on account of his flaw are not tragic. The fatal flaw here is in the misinterpretation of Aristotle, not in any tragedy or in anything Aristotle said about them.

Aristotle says and repeats that the downfall of the tragic figure is not from any vice or badness of character but from some *hamartia*, some great *hamartia* (1053a 8-10, 15-16). If a flaw is a small blemish of character, and Aristotle says that the tragic downfall is not from badness of character at all, and is from something that is not small, one hardly needs to know any Greek to see that the one thing Aristotle cannot mean by *hamartia* is a flaw. Unfortunately, though, there are English versions of the *Poetics* that translate that word in that way. In the English-speaking world, the mistranslation seems to trace its authority to S. H. Butcher's book *Aristotle's Theory of Poetry and Fine Art*, first published in 1895 and influential for half a century;

Butcher mentions a flaw of character as one of three meanings *hamartia* can have, though he himself translates its uses in the *Poetics* as "error or frailty." Still, since Aristotle says in the passage we are discussing that the tragic figure is not someone "surpassing in virtue and justice," one might think that his general idea must be that the character of such a person is flawed. But there may be a considerable difference between being something other than perfect and having a flawed perfection.

The two adjectives Aristotle uses in the *Poetics* for the character of the tragic figure are "decent" (*epieikês*) and "solid" or "trustworthy" (*chrêstos*). The word he pointedly avoids using for that character is *spoudaios*, which he uses throughout the *Nicomachean Ethics* for the person of shining excellence, though he speaks often even there of the virtues of ordinary decent people. Chapter 2 of the *Poetics* begins by distinguishing tragedy and comedy as imitations of the two extremes of character, but immediately and repeatedly replaces that distinction with one between people better or worse than "we" or "those of our sort" or "people as they are now" (1448a 4, 5, 17-18). Chapter 3 distinguishes the manner of imitating action as drama or narrative, and leads to the shift Aristotle makes when he comes to define tragedy in Chapter 6: it is not the person but the action itself that is *spoudaios* (1449b 24), of serious moral stature and at the highest limit of human striving. The person who chooses it is solidly decent, in the middle range between badness and surpassing goodness, but toward the better end of that range (1453a 7, 16-17). Nothing in that account suggests moral perfection with one blemish.

The word *hamartia* is used in many ways, but its root sense, and the image that is never absent from its metaphorical extensions, is that of missing a mark with a spear or an arrow. No ancient Greek brought up on the *Iliad* would ever hear the word without that resonance. If the idea of the "tragic flaw" is that the central figure by some lapse does some uncharacteristically bad thing, then that idea turns Aristotle's account of tragedy upside down.[3] There is no tragedy, according to Aristotle, unless a characteristically good central figure is aiming at something exceptionally high. For there to be a *hamartia*, there must first be a mark to be missed. And in the *Nicomachean Ethics*, Aristotle has even told us in a general way what that mark is, in saying that all the virtues of character aim at action that is beautiful in itself (1115b

---

3   A brief passage in Ch. 18 (1456a 19-25) has puzzled or misled many interpreters. It is the only place in the *Poetics* in which Aristotle speaks of flawed characters, and his two examples are of seriously flawed people who get their just deserts, to the delight of the audience. He says that poets like to tell such stories and tell them wonderfully well, and that they have something tragic about them. But what they share with tragedy is only the depiction of suffering; they lack the essential ingredients of pity and fear. The passage in no way changes anything said in Ch. 13.

12-13, 1122b 6-7). Achieving such an end is what Aristotle also calls "hitting the mean" (1106b 15-16, 27-28), where he pairs the word for hitting a target (*stochastikê*) directly with a form of the word *hamartia* (1106b 28-29), and makes clear that such a mean is an extreme of excellence (1107a 7-8, 23). In the opening scene of Sophocles' *Philoctêtês* (lines 94-95), Neoptolemus hits precisely on this aspect of the choice that makes tragedy possible: "I would rather miss the mark in a beautiful action than win a victory through a bad one." Forms of the word *hamartia* are used more than once in each of the seven surviving plays of Sophocles, and at least thirty-four times in them all.

It is widely noted in discussions of the *Poetics* that Aristotle uses the notion of *hamartia* in the *Nicomachean Ethics* for a special kind of harm that is neither accidental nor malicious (1135a 15-b 25), brought about by someone whose action is not involuntary but not wholly voluntary either (1110b 18-1111a 21). In the one passage, his focus is on blameworthy acts of negligence, while in the other it is on forgivable acts of ignorance. The tragic deed is somehow both, and the one who does and suffers it is both a responsible agent and an innocent victim. The examples given in the two *Ethics* passages overlap, and include one from a play by Euripides, one from the life of Aeschylus, and one of an unnamed man who strikes someone he does not know is his father, though he knows he is a human being. This last is not the action that forms Sophocles' *Oedipus Tyrannus*, but it is narrated in it (800-813), and plays an important part in revealing Oedipus's character. It is easy to assume that it shows what a hothead he is, and for anyone hunting for a tragic flaw, that tells the whole story. It happens, though, that Aristotle himself tells a different story in the *Nicomachean Ethics*.

The two passages that explore the complexities in the notion of *hamartia* are both followed by discussions of actions that arise out of spiritedness (*thumos*). In one of them, Aristotle mentions that such actions can be beautiful (1111a 27-29), and in the other, he says that the harm that may come from them is the fault of the one who insulted the spirited person (1135b 25-1136a 1). The sort of insult Aristotle has in mind is *hubris*, which he defines in the *Rhetoric* (Bk. II, Chap. 2) as a belittling of another for the sheer pleasure of causing pain through shame. Such a belittling may be directed also at the other person's family, friends, homeland, or race, and the natural response to it is spirited anger. In the *Nicomachean Ethics* (1149a 24-b 23), Aristotle argues that even someone who is too hasty in taking offense and revenge is to be forgiven for a natural and open-hearted response, and concludes by observing that there is no *hubris* in spiritedness. In this passage, he mentions two examples of sons who beat their fathers. It is reasonable to ask how he would interpret Oedipus's unknowing killing of his father.

As that event is narrated in *Oedipus Tyrannus*, Oedipus is alone on a highway, walking with a staff because he has been lame since infancy. An old man in a chariot, attended by four servants, rides up on him, and has the men and horses continue forward, forcing Oedipus off the road; he strikes back in anger at the charioteer. The old man, watching for a clear shot, hits Oedipus squarely on the head with his cattle prod. Oedipus instantly lashes back with his staff, knocking the old man onto the ground. In the ensuing fight with three remaining servants (one having run away) and the old man himself, Oedipus kills them all. The language of the passage suggests that the man in the road is being treated like an animal, that he is always attacked by at least two against one, and that this brutal and demeaning treatment is deliberate while the violence of his reaction springs up in the heat of the moment. As an anonymous victim of high-handed force, Oedipus is reacting in defense of outraged humanity. The conventional view that anger equals flaw equals *hubris* is not Aristotle's view. His opinion, plainly stated and directly applicable to this scene, is that, in an act such as Oedipus's, anger is spiritedness, human nature is displayed, and forgiveness is called for. All the *hubris* is on the other side, and it is a direct affront to human decency.

Oedipus's lashing out in anger at arrogant and brutal men, in ignorance of who they are and heedlessness of any consequences that may follow, is not a model of a tragic action, because it is not an action stemming from choice. The tragedy is shaped by his decision to save Thebes from a plague by taking the city to or into himself (*eruomai*, 72) and destroying its destroyer, a deliberate choice in which thought, the desires of a decent person, and spiritedness all converge in one aim. Oedipus pushes forward at great speed, trying to outthink those he says are scheming against him (618-619), using the same word Aristotle uses in the *Nicomachean Ethics* (1149b 14) to defend the too-spirited person for being "no schemer" (*epiboulos*). The chorus in *Oedipus Tyrannus* urges Oedipus to take Creon's beautiful advice to be cautious and play it safe (616-617), but he replies that if he remained calm, his effort to save the things he holds dear would run a greater risk of *hamartia*.

Katharsis

The missing of the mark, by a good person attempting to do something admirable, is what carries the spectator from fear to pity. The result that this accomplishes is described by Aristotle first as a *katharsis* of such feelings (1449b 27-28). This one use of this one word has given rise to the richest and most extensive discussion of the *Poetics* in the secondary literature, partly because Aristotle gives no explanation of it but partly because it is such a powerful metaphor that people are led to seek in it the meaning of their own powerful experience in response to tragedies. I believe that the word drops out of the subsequent unfolding of the *Poetics* because it is replaced by other words that Aristotle considers more precise and more revealing, but he clearly wants us to come to those other notions only by thinking first about *katharsis*.

Our English word catharsis is descended from the Greek word, but the descendant carries a weight of history that it gathered long after Aristotle used its ancestor. We know what it is to experience a catharsis, a clearing of the air that releases pent-up feelings. This has been the dominant interpretation of Aristotle's meaning at least since Jacob Bernays wrote in 1857 (in one part of what later appeared as *Two Essays on the Aristotelian Theory of Drama*) that dramatic catharsis is a therapeutic purgation, relieving oppressive emotions by arousing and expelling them. Change the word "oppressive" to "repressed" and you can see the influential boost given to this interpretation by a certain nephew by marriage of Bernays, named Sigmund Freud. But an older tradition looked at the function of poetic literature not as therapeutic simply but as educative, as a cultivation and elevation of sensibility. John Milton, writing in 1671 (Preface to *Samson Agonistes*), takes Aristotle to mean that the power of tragedies "to purge the mind" of pity and fear "is, to temper and reduce them to just measure." This sort of purging is like the refining of a precious metal by melting away impurities. In the 1760s (*Hamburgische Dramaturgie*, No. 78), G. E. Lessing takes just this line in calling the *katharsis* a purification that transmutes passions into virtues, in the strict sense of leading the soul away from both sentimental excesses and unfeeling defects of pity and fear.

These senses of purgation and refinement are both present in the Greek word, but a stronger meaning it has is a ritual purification from some polluting impiety. In fact, the only time Aristotle uses the word *katharsis* or any form of it in the *Poetics* outside its one appearance in the definition of tragedy is in a reference to the purification of a religious statue in a play of Euripides (1455b 15). But taking this meaning as primary has led a couple of twentieth-century scholars (H. Otte, G. Else) to the most implausible of all the interpretations of the tragic *katharsis*. They have understood it as an event not in the spectator at all but within the drama, in which the central figure first incurs and then somehow is purified of moral guilt. This approach never caught on, but there is yet another novel way of interpreting the *katharsis* that is enjoying a good deal of current acceptance, according to which the word comes into the *Poetics* directly from Plato's *Sophist*. In that dialogue, the notion is entertained that sophistry might belong together with de-lousing as an art that separates something worse from something better, the latter on bodies and the former in souls (226A-231B). Sophistry, in its unlimited capacity to refute any belief as well as its opposite, could be viewed as a preparatory education of the intellect, accomplishing a clearing-out (*katharsis*) of all opinions that anyone mistakes for knowledge. The scholar (Leon Golden) who came up with this reading of the *Poetics* just needed to change "clearing-out" to "clarification" to make the tragic *katharsis* a process belonging solely to the intellect. Another scholar (Martha Nussbaum) follows him part-way, though she understands that feelings are integral to the *katharsis*; she nudges the word back a half-step to "clearing-up," as of moral confusion or obscured insight.

None of these four main understandings of the *katharsis* brought about by a tragedy is wholly adequate. There may well be a purgation of feelings, in two ways. The drama may arouse painful but thrilling feelings and leave us feeling better afterward, because the pain passes off harmlessly and the thrill was without risk. For this sort of vicarious self-indulgence, though, horror movies and tear-jerkers are far more effective than tragedies. But also, the fear and pity felt in response to a tragedy may attach themselves to free-floating feelings of anxiety or depression that are already in us, and carry them away too; this sort of psycho-therapeutic effect may be a more serious thing than the first kind of purging, but it is still so generic an experience that it leaves any special response peculiar to tragedy unexplained. The same difficulty attends the notion that tragedies refine and elevate our feelings, even if they incidentally do so, and the power of tragedy seems to be something that can affect the young and old, educated and uneducated, and refined and coarse among its spectators equally. Next, if there is anything like a ritual purification enacted in a tragedy, it is hardly accomplished by means of pity and fear. And lastly, the idea that a tragedy brings about an intellectual clarification is dangerously close to saying it teaches a lesson; this view leaves one puzzled both at how pity and fear could be the means of such instruction, and at how so lame a conclusion measures up to everything a tragedy puts us through. But the modified version of clarification, according to which tragedy clears up our sight by somehow readjusting our feelings, perhaps comes the closest of all these accounts of *katharsis* to something Aristotle might be saying and tragedy might be doing.

One thing that tends to be lost or slighted in all the literature about *katharsis* is the root sense of washing or cleansing that gives it its force as a metaphor. Aristotle tells us that the imitation of an action in a tragedy, by means of the fear and pity it makes us feel, ends in a cleansing of feelings of that sort. His choice to call these cleansed feelings *pathêmata* rather than *pathê* may be a way of pointing to the persisting feelings that result as distinct from the temporarily intense feelings that are the means to them. When Aristotle speaks later of the fear and pity that are aroused in the first place, he calls them *pathê* (1456a 38-b 1). But what sense could it make to say that feeling an acute fear for a couple of hours can leave behind an altered and cleansed persistent kind of fear? And the question seems equally strange when asked about pity. Perhaps the problem, though, is that we have not yet asked the question about fear and pity as united in one experience.

We have seen that it is the linkage of pity and fear in a tragedy that produces the image of a human being who is simultaneously the responsible cause and the innocent victim of destruction. We have seen too that this unity of ruin, responsibility, and blamelessness is produced only if the tragic figure reflects something good and decent in the humanity we share. Our feelings of fear tell us, with a gradually increasing sense of inevitability, that an original beautiful choice can have no good outcome, while the sense of undeserved suffering in our feelings of pity tell us that there was no decent way to avoid that choice. Two things, I think, are impossible at the end of a tragedy, if we are to do justice to the whole of what we feel. Our pity cannot stand alone as a sense of the unfairness or unspeakable ugliness of it all, and our fear cannot prompt us to feel that a wrongdoer has been taught a lesson. Our fear, directed at something good in the tragic figure that we share, cuts off any wallowing in sentimental pity. Our pity, insisting on the undeserved nature of the suffering, blocks any relief in indignant moralism. Oedipus's ruin is his own doing, but not his fault; his missing of the mark is a great sorrow, but also a beautiful choice. Each of the two feelings works on the other, and leaves it changed. This is not a refinement of sensibility that makes our feelings subtler and less coarse; it is a direct and solid impact of two forces that any human being can feel. It does not clear pity and fear out of our systems, but leaves them with us in a strange new combination. By no means does it clear anything up. It calls for clarification and denies us any easy access to it. What is the moral of *Oedipus Tyrannus*? It has none that does not cheapen our full experience of the play. Is it perhaps possible to see this result as washing our pity clean of sentimentality and our fear clean of self-righteousness? I am not sure how to answer that question. I may be reaching to make too many things fit, but if this interpretation of *katharsis*, like all the others, seems to miss the mark, doesn't Aristotle himself hit the mark simply in saying that at the end of a tragedy we feel washed?

Wonder

If Aristotle had done nothing but apply the metaphor of *katharsis* to the final result of a tragedy, he would have made a great contribution to our thinking about it. The interpretation and counter-interpretation his word has inspired is all valuable. Drama does provoke and relieve strong feelings. Fiction does disclose to us new and higher objects of those feelings. And poetry does in some way instruct and enlighten us. The rich and many-sided consideration of the ways tragedy does and does not include these effects deepens our thinking about all imaginative literature. Even completely misguided commentary, of which there is much that I have not mentioned, helps us by exposing its own errors to the light of day, but the commentary I have discussed all gets hold from some angle of something that is present in tragedy, in Aristotle's account of it, and in our lives. But we are not left unguided in this salutary field of exploration that Aristotle opened up to us. As I have mentioned, *katharsis* is not his last word on the effect of tragedy, and he may well have intended it to stir up this very array of possibilities so that we might recognize his return to the subject as taking us a step beyond them all.

The reference to *katharsis* is in Chapter 6, in Aristotle's summing up of his preliminary review of the parts of a tragedy; the next five chapters explore its wholeness. This is found to require a single central character and a coherence that comes from the sort of person that character is imagined to be, rather than from any source in legends (1451a 24-30) or imitation of history (1451b 4-5), but first of all, it requires that events be put together in such a way that the end comes out of the beginning either by necessity or as it would for the most part; this gives the story a wholeness like that of a living thing, and opens up the possibility of beauty (1450b 29-37). Eight times in Chapters 7-11, Aristotle refers to this need for necessary or likely sequence. Lacking this kind of sequence, what happens on the stage is merely episodic (1451b 33-37); it might be entertaining, but it is not tragedy. On the other hand, the mere unfolding of expected consequences is hardly a tragedy either, or not much of one. The crucial element, Aristotle says, in producing or enhancing fear and pity, is that the necessary or likely sequence should come about paradoxically (*para tên doxan*, 1452a 1-4). And in the reason he gives, we finally arrive one step beyond *katharsis*. The combination of a necessary or likely sequence with a paradoxical outcome will inevitably produce a more beautiful tragedy, he says, because it will be more a source of wonder.

We have already seen that the combination of fear and pity in a tragedy means that we take the same person at once as responsible for and an undeserving victim of his own destruction, and that we feel that, in missing the mark he aims at, he is both guilty and innocent. This is a paradox, but it is not enough by itself to give rise to tragedy. The stories about King Midas make him responsible for destructive effects of which he is also the victim, but his daughter and his food don't turn into gold through any necessary or likely sequence of action. The paradoxical fusion of innocence and guilt in a tragedy comes about *naturally*. Aristotle's first and fullest description of a likely result is as what follows something else naturally and for the most part (1450b 28-30). In the *Physics* (198b 34-36), Aristotle treats the second of these two qualifications, what happens for the most part, as a sufficient sign of the first, what happens by nature. The wonder Aristotle attributes to tragedy is evoked not by an artificially contrived clever story, but by the naturalness of its imitation of an action. It is thus akin, if not identical, to the wonder that might arise in response to certain events we experience in nature itself.

Near the beginning of the *Metaphysics*, Aristotle speaks of sources of wonder, and gives as his first examples things that happen to the moon, the sun, and the stars (982b 15-16, 983a 15). The moon and sun are occasionally eclipsed. Every summer and winter the sun stops and reverses its course up and down the sky. And periodically every one of the planets stops and reverses its eastward course through the fixed stars. In each of these instances, a recognizable and expected sequence of events leads to a surprising result, not by chance or miraculous intervention, but out of the natural course of things. Tragedy is akin to these foreseeable but always surprising spectacles in nature. Aristotle says of the wonder that comes from nature that it leads to the activity of philosophy, echoing the famous claim of Socrates in the *Theaetetus* that wonder is the only beginning of philosophy (155C). But neither of them is talking about curiosity, or the mere noticing of a difficulty that makes one say "I wonder how that happened." Socrates also describes the beginning of philosophy in the form of a parable about Thales, the first philosopher, who while looking at the stars fell into a well. This is a potent wonder, an experience in which the ground drops away from under one's feet.

In the *Poetics*, Aristotle describes the experience of wonder with a word that carries a metaphoric meaning equivalent to that in Socrates's parable. He says that when something unknown becomes known in a tragedy, out of the action itself and in a likely way, its effect is to knock something away from us (1455a 16-17). His word is *ekplêxis*, which is usually translated as astonishment, but the metaphor in that English word is a turning into stone, while the Greek word points instead to a loss of some sort of support. In the next-to-last chapter of the *Poetics*, Aristotle uses the adjective *ekplêktikos*, having the power to knock something away from us, as a description of the end of the art of poetry itself, without which it misses its mark (1460b 22-26). It follows that producing wonder is not some sort of occasional consequence of tragedy, but the very thing at which it aims; and Aristotle says exactly this in Chapter 24 (1460a 11-12). That claim amounts to nothing less than the long-delayed completion of the definition of tragedy that began eighteen chapters earlier. The *katharsis*, the washing away, is more aptly described as an *ekplêxis*, a knocking away, and the state in which we are left is wonder.

The fact that Aristotle considered the effect of tragedy to be wonder was well known to the writers of the middle ages and the Renaissance. It was also well known to the twentieth-century poet and scholar J. V. Cunningham, whose 1951 book *Woe or Wonder* (Chap. IV) brilliantly traces the connection of wonder with tragedy from Aristotle's *Poetics* though an unbroken tradition leading to the plays of Shakespeare. But nowhere in the current secondary literature about the *Poetics* have I found a single indication of an awareness that Cunningham's book exists. That literature scarcely notes in passing that wonder is even mentioned in the *Poetics*, and when it does so, it is merely as part of a justification for saying that tragedy has an intellectual content. The only explanation I can think of for this lack of attention is that wonder itself has ceased to be considered important in our time. More precisely, the so-called scientific revolution of the seventeenth century demoted wonder. Rene Descartes, in the 1646 book *The Passions of the Soul* (Part II, Article LXXVI), wrote "we wonder too much...And this may entirely prevent or pervert the use of reason. That is why, although it is good to be born with some inclination towards this passion, because that disposes us for the acquisition of the sciences, we must at the same time afterwards try to free ourselves from it as much as possible." If we already have the framework in which all truth is to be found, wonder is at best superfluous, and at worst subversive.

What is characteristic of wonder is the sudden loss of the sense that we understand what is going on. What it knocks away are all our habitual assumptions and opinions. In the state of wonder we are not fitting what is in front of us into the explanatory structures that normally guide our lives, but are in the rare condition of taking in the things before us just as they are. There is a paradigm of this experience near the end of the *Iliad*, when Priam and Achilles momentarily cease to be enemies, or even suppliant and benefactor, and gaze at each other in wonder, each just seeing the human being in front of him (Bk. 24, 628-633). And if our earlier discussion of *katharsis* was on the right track, the impact of a tragedy is to leave us gazing at a human image with our habits of blaming and excusing blocked. We are not left saying "he got what he deserved," but we can't say either that he was a helpless victim of a heartless or hideous universe. The poet has knocked all our moralism and sentimentality out of us.

But it does not follow that the poet has taught us anything. His impact is on our feelings, and we can recover our usual habits of judging as soon as those feelings wear off. We might begin to think more deeply, but even if wonder is the only beginning of philosophy, it is by no means true that philosophy is the only outcome of wonder. Aristotle notes in the *Poetics* that wonder is a pleasure (1460a 17), and we may merely enjoy it while it lasts like any other pleasure to be found at the theater. What seems to me wrong at bottom with the interpretations that stop at *katharsis* and never get as far as wonder is that they imply that tragedy brings about in each of us a single necessary final result. Wonder, on the other hand, is not necessarily a final result at all but an opportunity, and it doesn't bring home any one kind of lesson or improvement. The state of wonder holds in abeyance for an extended moment the natural flow of our opinions. That is an amazing gift that the world or a poet can sometimes give us, but if anything is to come of it, it will have to be our own doing. We noted at the start that anything that happens to us can melt away, and lose any chance to remain within our experience, if we do not reflect upon it. Tragedy, in Aristotle's view of it, is an opportunity for such reflection, and an invitation to the most serious kind of change we can undergo.

My first effort to put together thoughts about the whole of Aristotle's *Poetics* was a lecture called "Tragic Pleasure," published in the *St. John's Review* XLIII, 1 (1995) and also available online through the Internet Encyclopedia of Philosophy. Some parts of that study took their bearings in important ways from things I learned from Bill O'Grady, whose remarkable power as a teacher continues undiminished by his untimely death. Everything I wrote then still seems true to me, but I have now come to see one decisive thing about the relation of pity and fear that has carried my understanding of the work to a new place. That insight, new to me, was argued by my friend and colleague John White in his introduction to a summer discussion of the *Poetics* sometime in the late 1970s or early 1980s. I remember vividly his claim that we feel pity for the blinded Oedipus and fear him at the same moment, and similarly with Achilles when, in Bk. XVIII of the *Iliad* (lines 215-231), he shouts a war-cry that is simultaneously an outpouring of his grief. With equal vividness I remember my thought that while that sounded right and important, it could not be what Aristotle intended, since he describes the tragic response of fear as directed at the things or people threatening the character we later pity, once our fears come true. What I could not bring into focus for myself then was what I now see is the central paradox of tragedy. Oedipus himself grapples with it in *Oedipus at Colonus* (lines 266-7) when he says "my deeds are more things suffered than things done," and Shakespeare's *King Lear* echoes him twenty or so centuries later in claiming to be "a man more sinned against than sinning." I see now too that a dim sense of this paradox has always guided my thinking about tragedies, giving me confidence that Oedipus is not gratuitously violent, that Othello is not a man easily jealous, or that Macbeth does have in him the milk of human kindness, even though none of these figures is blameless either for the wreckage he brings about. Tragedy would not be tragedy if our fear of and pity for the destruction of a worthy human being did not finally fuse with a fear of something in that same person. Aristotle has seen to the heart of a complex imaginative experience, and John White had got hold of what was most crucial to it. I am pleased, some quarter of a century after I heard him articulate that, to find it the source of a new depth and clarity in my own learning.

I am grateful to John White also for introducing me to the writings of J. V. Cunningham. No published work has influenced my understanding of the *Poetics* more than Cunningham's nearly unknown study *Woe or Wonder*, which is included in the book *Tradition and Poetic Structure* (Swallow Press, 1960). A translation of Jacob Bernays' influential interpretation of tragic catharsis can be found in the collection *Articles on Aristotle IV*, edited by Barnes et al. (Duckworth, 1979). The incidental details of Bernays' considerable classical scholarship are as valuable to think about as are his central claims. A collection of good recent commentary is *Essays on Aristotle's Poetics*, edited by A. O. Rorty (Princeton U. P., 1992), and two of the most interesting interpretations can be pursued further in Leon Golden's *Aristotle on Tragic and Comic Mimesis* (Scholar's Press, 1992) and Martha Nussbaum's *The Fragility of Goodness* (Cambridge U. P., 1986).

The present translation is made from the Oxford Classical Text of the *Poetics* (1965), and the numbers given between the indications of the standard Bekker pages refer to its lines. As always, I have assumed that the reader wants to get as close as possible to what Aristotle wrote, and is willing to make some effort of thought to achieve that, but this is not at all what is usually called literal translation. There is no one-to-one correspondence between the contents of contemporary English and those of Aristotle's Greek, but his ways of saying things can be approximated, and I have done my best to capture them without falling into needless unclarity.

Annapolis, Maryland

Winter, 2005

POETICS

Chapter 1

1447a About the poetic art itself and the forms of it, what specific capacity each has, and how one ought to put together stories[4] if the making of them is going to hold together beautifully, and also how many and **10** what sort of parts stories are made of, and likewise about as many other things as belong to the inquiry into poetic art, let us speak once we have first started, in accord with nature, from the things that come first.

Now epic poetry and the making of tragedy, and also comedy and dithyrambic poetry, as well as most flute-playing and lyre-playing, are all as a whole just exactly imitations, but they are different from one another in three ways, for they differ either by making their imitations in different things, by imitating different things, or by imitating differently and not in the same way. For just as some people who make images imitate many things by means of both colors and shapes (some **20** through art and others through habituation), and others by means of the voice, so too with the arts mentioned, all of them make imitations in rhythm, speech, and harmony,[5] and with these

---

4   The words for the poetic art (*hê poiêtikê*) and for poetry (*poiêsis*) are first of all general names for any art or process of making. This same usage is present in English in the title of the Scottish 15th or 16th century poem *Lament for the Makers* by William Dunbar. Aristotle's assumption is that poetic making is primarily a making of stories. The connection of stories with making is also present in English in the word fiction.

5   *Harmonia* could mean music in general, but had the primary meaning of a fitting or joining together of parts. The more musical forms of poetry joined more elements with metered speech, in some cases an instrumental accompaniment, in others dancing or an elaboration of metrical patterns. Dithyrambs combined song, dance, prologues spoken in meter, and flute ensembles, and sometimes even fitted in metrical dialogue. (See also footnote 7.)

either separate or mixed. For example, both flute-playing and lyre-playing, and any other arts there happen to be that are of that sort in their capacity, such as the art of the Pan-pipes, use only harmony and rhythm, while the art of dancers uses rhythm itself apart from harmony (for they too, through the rhythms of their gestures, imitate states of character, feelings, and actions). But the art that uses bare words and the one that uses meters, and the latter either **1447b** mixing meters with one another or using one particular kind, happen to be nameless up to now. For we **10** have nothing to use as a name in common for the mimes of Sophron and Xenarchus and the Socratic dialogues, even if someone were to make the imitation with [iambic] trimeters or elegiac [couplets] or anything else of that sort. Instead, people connect the poetic making with the meter and name "elegiac poets," or others "epic poets," calling them poets not as a result of the imitation but as a result of the meter as what is common to them, for even when they bring out something medical or about nature in meter, people are accustomed to speak of them in that way. But nothing is common to Homer and Empedocles except the meter, and hence, while it is just to call the former a poet, the latter is more a student of nature than a poet. **20** By the same token, even if someone were to make an imitation by mixing all the meters, the very way Chaeremon made the *Centaur* as a patchwork mixture of all the meters, one would have to call him too a poet. As for these things,[6] then, let them be distinguished in this way. And there are some arts that use all the things mentioned—I mean, for instance, rhythm and melody and meter—as do the making of both dithyrambs and nomes,[7] and both tragedy and comedy.

---

6   Things having to do with the medium in which the imitation is made. Chapters 2 and 3 deal, respectively, with what is imitated and the manner in which it is imitated.

7   In contrast to the wilder dithyramb involved in the worship of Dionysus, the nome was a more stately choral ode danced and sung in honor of Apollo.

Chapter 2

1448a Since those doing the imitating imitate people acting, and it is necessary that the latter be people either of serious moral stature or of a low sort (for states of character pretty much always follow these sorts alone, since all people differentiate states of character by vice and virtue), they imitate either those better than we are or worse, or else of our sort, just as painters do. For Polygnotus used to make images of superior people, Pauson of inferior, and Dionysius of those like us. And it is clear too that each of the kinds of imitation mentioned will have these differences and will be different by imitating different things in this manner. For even in dance, in flute-playing, and **10** in lyre-playing, it is possible for these dissimilarities to be brought into being, as well as in what involves speeches and meters bare of music, as Homer imitated better people, Cleophon people similar to us, and Hegemon the Thasian, who first made parodies, and Nicochares, who made the *Timidiad*, imitated worse people. And similarly as concerns dithyrambs and nomes, one might make imitations in the same ways Timotheus and Philoxenus each made his *Cyclops*. And by this very difference tragedy stands apart in relation to comedy, for the latter intends to imitate those who are worse, and the former better, than people are now.

Chapter 3

Yet a third of these differences is how one might imitate **20** each of these things. For it is also possible to imitate the same things, in the same things, sometimes by narrating—either becoming a particular other, as Homer does, or as the same [narrative voice] and not changing—or with all those doing the imitating performing deeds and being in activity. So the imitation is present in these three differences, as we said at the beginning: the in which, the what, and the how. As a result, Sophocles is in one sense the same sort of imitator as

Homer, since both imitate people of serious moral stature, but in another sense Sophocles is the same sort of imitator as Aristophanes, since they both imitate with people performing deeds and acting [*drôntas*]. And this is why some people say the latter are called dramas, because they imitate with people acting. For this reason too **30** the Dorians take credit for both tragedy and comedy (for the Megarians there take credit for comedy as having come into being at the time of their democracy, as do the Megarians in Sicily, since Epicharmus the poet was from there, being much earlier than Chionides and Magnes, and some of those in the Peloponnese take credit for tragedy). They make the names a sign of this, for they say they call their rural villages *cômai* while the Athenians call them *dêmoi*, and that comic actors were so called not from their reveling (*comazein*) but for their wandering from village to village, since they were banned in dishonor from the city. **1448b** And they call performing an action *dran* while Athenians call it *prattein*. So about the differences among imitations, both how many and what they are, let these things have been said.

Chapter 4

And it is likely that two particular causes, and these natural ones, brought into being the poetic art as a whole. For imitating is co-natural with human beings from childhood, and in this they differ from the other animals because they are the most imitative and produce their first acts of understanding by means of imitation; also all human beings take delight in imitations. A sign of this is what happens **10** in our actions, for we delight in contemplating the most accurately made images of the very things that are painful for us to see, such as the forms of the most contemptible insects and of dead bodies. What is responsible even for this is that understanding is most pleasant not only for philosophers but in a similar way for everyone else, though they share in it to a short extent. They delight in seeing images for this reason: because understanding and reasoning out what each thing is results when they contemplate them, for instance "that's who this is," since if one happens not to have seen him before, the image will not produce pleasure as an imitation, but only on account of its workmanship or coloring or for some other such reason.

20 Since imitating is in accord with our nature, as harmony and rhythm are (for it is evident that meters are parts of rhythms), from the beginning those who were naturally disposed toward these things the most, progressing little by little, brought the poetic art into being out of their improvised performances. And the making of poetry split apart in accordance with their own characters, for the more dignified poets imitated beautiful actions and people of the sort who perform them, while the less worthy sort imitated actions of low people, first making abusive poems just as the others made hymns and praises. Of the former, while we have no such poem to speak of from anyone before Homer, it is likely that there were many, but starting from Homer **30** there are many, such as his *Margites* [8] and things of that sort. In them, as fitting to them, the iambic meter came in; that is why they are even now called iambic poems, because it is in this meter that they used to ridicule (*iambizein*) one another. And some of the ancients became makers of heroic poetry, others of iambic. But just as Homer most of all was the poet for things of serious stature (because not only did he make his imitations well in other respects, but he made them dramatic), so too he was the first to indicate the pattern of comedy, not as abusive but as dramatizing what is ridiculous. [9] For the *Margites* has an analogous position: as the *Iliad* **1449a** and the *Odyssey* are to tragedies, so too is it to comedies. And when tragedy and comedy had come to sight next to each other, once those who

---

8   A lost poem no longer believed to be by Homer. In the *Nicomachean Ethics* (1141a 15-16), Aristotle quotes a description of its central character: "The gods made him neither a ditchdigger nor a plowman, nor wise in any other respect."

9   That is, he displayed in a dramatic image something ridiculous in human beings or human types in general, rather than ridiculing particular actual people.

had made a start, in accord with their own natures, toward each sort of poetry, some became makers of comedies instead of iambic poems, others author-directors of tragedies instead of makers of epics, because these forms were more full-grown and worthier than those.

Now to examine whether tragedy is, therefore, already in good enough shape in its forms or not, in order to judge it both in itself and in relation to its audiences, is another story. But since it came into being from an improvisational **10** origin—both it and comedy, the former from those who began the dithyramb, the latter from those who began the phallic songs which even now still continue to be customary in many cities—tragedy grew little by little as people made progress in as much of it as had become evident. And when tragedy had gone through many changes it came to rest, since it had hold of its nature. Aeschylus first brought the number of actors from one to two, reduced the parts belonging to the chorus, and made speech take the primary place; Sophocles provided three actors and painted scenery. Also there is its magnitude; out of little stories and **20** ridiculous wording—since it changed out of the satyr-play—it has lately become dignified, and the meter, from [trochaic] tetrameter, has become iambic. At first they used the tetrameter because the poetry was suited to the satyr-play and more appropriate for dancing,[10] but when talking came in, nature itself found the meter it was at home in, for the iambic is the most speakable of the meters. A sign of this is that we talk mostly in iambs in conversation with one another but in hexameters seldom and as departures from an inflection[11] suited to talking. Also there

---

10   Longfellow's *Song of Hiawatha* ("By the shores of Gitche Gumee...") and Poe's *The Raven* ("Once upon a midnight dreary...") are English poems in trochaic tetrameter. Meters in English are based on stress accents rather than syllable length, but these examples may give some indication of the rapid, headlong quality of that meter.

11   "Inflection" here translates *harmonia*, which has been translated as harmony up to now. Hexameters give English a sing-song or chant-like tone, as in Longfellow's *Evangeline* ("This is the forest primeval. The murmuring pines and the hemlocks... ") or Yeats's *The Wanderings of Oisin* ("The immortal desire of Immortals we saw in their faces and sighed...").

is the number of episodes. As for the other things that **30** each by each are said to have ornamented tragedy, let them be passed over by us with a mention, since it would perhaps be a lot of work to go through each in particular.

Chapter 5

Comedy, as we said, is an imitation of people of a lower sort, though not in respect to every vice; rather, what is ridiculous is part of what is ugly. For the ridiculous is a certain sort of missing the mark and a deformity that is painless and not destructive; an immediate example is the comic mask, which is something deformed and misshapen without causing pain. The changes of tragedy and the things through which it came into being have not gone unnoticed, but comedy, since it was not **1449b** taken seriously, went unnoticed from the beginning. And it was only recently when the archon[12] granted a chorus of comic players; before that they were only volunteers. But it is when comedy already had certain forms that those called poets of it were memorialized. Who gave it masks or prologues or a number of actors and everything of that sort is not to be known. The making of stories came first from Sicily, but among those in Athens, Crates first began taking away the look of personal ridicule to make speeches and stories that were universal.

Now epic poetry goes along with tragedy up to the point **10** of being an imitation in speech with meter of things of serious stature, but in respect to having a single meter and being a narration, in this respect they differ, as also in length. While the one tries as much as possible to be under one circuit of the sun or to vary little from it, epic poetry is indeterminate in time and differs in this respect, even though at first they used to do this the same way in tragedies as in epics. Some parts of them are the same, while others are peculiar to tragedy. On account

---

12   A government official in Athens who could approve applications from poets and assign a wealthy citizen to pay for a public performance. The actions of the archon were a matter of public record, so that comedy ceased to be "unnoticed."

of this, whoever knows about high- and low-quality tragedy knows about epics too, for what epic poetry has in it belongs to tragedy, while not all that belongs to the latter is in **20** epic poetry.

Chapter 6

About the art of imitating in hexameters and about comedy we will speak later.[13] But let us speak about tragedy, taking up again the definition of the kind of thing it is that comes into being out of what has been said. Tragedy, then, is an imitation of an action of serious stature and complete, having magnitude, in language made pleasing in distinct forms in its separate parts, imitating people acting and not using narration, accomplishing by means of pity and fear the cleansing of these states of feeling. By "language made pleasing" I mean that which has rhythm and harmony, and by "in distinct **30** forms" I mean accomplishing this in some parts through meters alone and in others in turn through song.[14] And since people engaged in action produce the imitation, the adornment of the spectacle would necessarily be a first component of a tragedy; next would be song-making and wording, since they make the imitation in these. By "wording" I mean the composition itself of the verses; as for song-making, the meaning it has is completely evident. And since tragedy is an imitation of an action, and action is performed by particular people engaged in action, who must necessarily be of some particular sort in both character and thinking, [and] it is natural for there to be two causes of actions, thinking and character[15] (for it is on account of these that **1450a** we say the actions too are of certain sorts, and as a result of *these* that everyone succeeds or fails), and the imitation of the action is the story

---

13   The first half of this promise is kept (in Chs. 23, 24, and 26), but the second half is not.

14   The choral odes, which alternated with scenes of dialogue, were in a combination of meters in elaborate patterns to be sung in accompaniment to the choral dance.

15   The position of the last clause, from the inserted word [and], varies in the manuscripts. The placement here is the translator's conjecture.

(since by "story" I mean this—the composition of the things done—while by "states of character" I mean that as a result of which we say the people who act are of certain particular sorts, and by "thinking" all those things they say in which they demonstrate something or even declare an opinion), then it is necessary that there be six parts of every tragedy, as a result of which the tragedy is of a particular sort. These are story, states of character, wording, **10** thinking, spectacle, and song-making.

Two parts are those in which they make the imitation, one the manner in which they imitate, and three are the things that they imitate, and there is none besides these. Not a few poets, so to speak, have used these as forms of tragedy, for even spectacle contains all of it, and character, story, wording, song, and thinking do so in the same way. But the greatest of these is the organization of the things done. For tragedy is an imitation not of people but of actions and life. Both happiness and wretchedness consist in action, and the end is a certain sort of action, not a quality[16]; while people are of certain sorts as a result of their characters, it is as a result of their **20** actions that they are happy or the opposite. Therefore, it is not that they act in order that they might imitate states of character; rather, they include states of character conjointly on account of the actions. So the actions performed and the story are the end of tragedy, and the end is the greatest of all things. Also, without action a tragedy could not come to be, but without states of character it could, for the tragedies of most of the new poets are characterless, and many poets generally are of that sort, the sort that Zeuxis also is inclined to be, among painters, as compared with Polygnotus. For while Polygnotus is good at depicting character, Zeuxis's painting has no character in it. Further, if one puts in a row phrases that show character, well made **30** in

---

16   The word "end" is used here in the sense it has in the phrase "ends and means" (as distinct from its use in the phrase "beginning, middle, and end" in Ch. 7) to indicate that for the sake of which something happens or exists, in this case human life. "Quality" translates the rare word *poiotês*, which means literally a "certain-sort*ness*."

both wording and thinking, he will not perform what was said to be the work of a tragedy, but the tragedy that uses these things in a more deficient way, but has a story and an organization of actions, will perform that work much more.

On top of these things, the greatest means by which tragedy draws the soul are parts of the story, namely reversals and discoveries. A further sign of this is that even those attempting to be poets have the capacity to be precise in wording and states of character earlier than in organizing the actions, as did just about all the first poets. The story, then, is the source and is like the soul of the tragedy, and states of character rank second. (It is pretty much the same **1450b** in the art of painting as well, for if one were to dab on the most beautiful paints in a conglomeration, that would not give delight in the same way as if one had painted a white silhouette.) Tragedy is an imitation of action, and it is mostly on account of this that it is an image of the people acting.

Thinking ranks third; this is the ability to say the things that are involved in the situation and are fitting to it, which is exactly the task in the speeches that belong to the political and rhetorical arts, for the old poets made people speak in a political way, while those nowadays make them speak rhetorically.[17] It is a particular sort of character that shows of what sort the choice is; **10** hence character has nothing to do with speeches in which there is nothing of a general sort which the one speaking chooses or rejects. But thinking is present in speeches in which they demonstrate the way something is or is not or state some universal proposition. And wording ranks fourth. As was said before, I mean by wording the conveying by words

---

17   This appears to be explained in the *Rhetoric*, where 1417a 16-36 is closely connected with the present passage. Aristotle says that the rhetoricians of his day spoke exclusively from thinking, which reveals practical judgment and what is advantageous, rather than from virtue, which, by its choice of an end beautiful in itself, reveals good character. As an example of the latter (presumably more political) way of speaking, he cites a speech of Antigone, lines 911-912 of Sophocles' play, an irrational defense of her choice to care more for her brother than for anyone or anything else.

of a meaning which has the same force whether it is in metrical verses or in speeches. Of the remaining components of tragedy, song-making is the greatest of the things by which it is made pleasing, and the spectacle, while it is able to draw the soul, is the component most foreign to the art and least inherent in poetry. For the power of tragedy is present even without a crowd of spectators and even without actors; what is more, the art of making masks and set decorations has more control over 20 bringing off the spectacle than does the art of the poets.

Chapter 7

Now that these distinctions have been made, let us say next of what sort the organization of the actions ought to be, since this is both the first and the greatest of the things that belong to tragedy. Now it has been set down by us that tragedy is an imitation of an action that is complete and whole and that has some magnitude, since it is possible for there to be a whole with no magnitude.[18] And a whole is that which has a beginning, middle, and end: a beginning is that which is not itself necessarily after anything else, but after which it is natural for another thing to be or come to be; an end is the opposite, something that is itself naturally after something else, either 30 necessarily or for the most part, with no other thing naturally after it; and a middle is that which is itself both after something else and has another thing after it. Therefore, well-organized stories must neither begin from wherever they may happen to nor end where they may happen to, but must have the look that has been described. Also, since what is beautiful, both an animal and every organized thing made of any parts, needs not only to have these arranged in an orderly way but also to start out with a magnitude that is not random (beauty consisting in magnitude as well as order), for that reason neither could a very tiny animal become beautiful (for the contemplation of it runs

---

18   In Bk. V, Ch. 26, of the *Metaphysics*, Aristotle says that any universal notion predicated of many particular things is a certain kind of whole.

together by coming about in a nearly imperceptible time) nor could one of huge magnitude (for the **1451a** contemplation of it could not come about all at once, but the unity and wholeness are swept away from its contemplation for those contemplating it), for instance if there should be an animal the length of ten thousand athletic fields.[19] So just as, in the case of bodies and of animals, they need to have magnitude, and this needs to be easily taken in view, so too, in the case of stories, they need to have a length, and this needs to be easily held in memory.

A limit of length that is determined by dramatic competitions and the viewing of them is no part of the art. For if a hundred tragedies needed to compete, they would be competing accompanied by water clocks, as people claim they did at some time or other. But in accord with the very **10** nature of the thing, the limit is that, as long as it is clearly taken in together, the larger thing is more beautiful in respect to magnitude. And determining it in a direct way, one may say that, in as great a magnitude as it takes for a change to happen into good from bad fortune, or from good to bad fortune, when it comes about by a likely or necessary sequence,[20] there is a sufficient limit of magnitude.

Chapter 8

A story is one, not, as some people suppose, if it is about one person, for many—countlessly many—things are incidental attributes of one person, with no unity taking in some of them. So too, there are many actions belonging to one person, out of which no one action comes about. For this reason, every

---

19   Literally stades, the length of the race track at the Olympic games, which became a standard measure.

20   This is the first linking in the *Poetics* of the words for what is necessary and what is likely. This pairing is repeated frequently in the following four chapters. But what is likely (*to eikos*) is explained above, in the account of beginnings, middles, and ends, as what happens naturally, when it does so not by invariable necessity but for the most part. In the *Physics* (198b 34-36), Aristotle treats the latter criterion as sufficient evidence that nature is at work. Likely sequence in the story, then, is an image of some aspect of nature working itself out in human action.

one of the **20** poets who has made a *Heracleid*, a *Theseid*, or other poems of that sort, has evidently missed the mark. For they suppose that since Heracles was one person, it is fitting that his story also be one story. But Homer, just as he excelled in other respects, also seems to have recognized this beautifully, whether by art or by nature. For in making an *Odyssey*, he did not make it out of all the things that happened to the man, such as being wounded on Parnassus, or pretending to be insane at the calling up of soldiers, things of which none was necessary or likely to happen because of another thing that happened, but the *Odyssey* is organized around one action of the sort we are speaking of, and similarly also with the *Iliad*. **30** So just as, in the other imitative arts, one imitation is of one thing, so too the story, since it is an imitation of an action, ought to be of one action and it ought to be a whole. And the parts of the actions performed ought to be organized in such a way that, when any part is displaced or removed, the whole becomes something different and changes. For that which makes no noticeable difference when it is there or not there is no part of the whole.

Chapter 9

And it is also evident from the things that have been said that the work of the poet is to speak not of things that have happened but of the sort of things that might happen and possibilities that come from what is likely or necessary. For the **1451b** historian and the poet differ not by speaking in metrical verse or without meter (for it would be possible to put the writings of Herodotus into meter, and they would be a history with meter no less than without it). Rather, they differ in this, that the one speaks of things that have happened, but the other of the sort of things that might happen. For this reason too, poetry is a more philosophical and more serious thing than history, since poetry speaks more of things that are universal, and history of things that are particular. It is what is universal, the sorts of things that a certain sort of person turns out to say or do as a result of what is likely or necessary, that **10** poetry aims at, even though it puts names on people. But what is particular is what Alcibiades did or what was done to him. Now in the case of comedy, this has already become clear, for once they have organized the story through things that are likely, they simply slip in random names, and do not make a story about a particular person, as did the poets of personal ridicule. In the case of tragedy, though, they hold on to the names that have come down to us. The reason is that what is possible is credible; we do not yet trust that things that have not happened are possible, but it is obvious that things that have happened are possible, since they could not have happened if they were impossible. Even in some tragedies, though, there are one **20** or two familiar names while the rest are made up, and in some there are none, as in Agathon's *Antheus*. In this tragedy the deeds and names alike are made up, and it gives no less delight. So holding on to the stories that have been passed down about those whom tragedies concern is not entirely something to be sought. To seek this would even be ridiculous, since even the familiar stories are familiar to few people, but they give delight to all people. In fact, it is clear from these things that the poet ought to be a poet more so of his stories than of his meters, in as much as he is a poet in virtue of imitation, and he imitates actions. And therefore it follows **30** that, in making a story out of things that have happened, he is no less a poet, since among the things that have happened, nothing prevents some from being of a sort that are likely to have happened, and he is a poet of those things in virtue of that.[21]

Of simple stories and actions, those that are episodic are worst. I call "episodic" a story in which the episodes coming one after another are neither likely nor necessary. Tragedies of this sort are made by low-grade poets on account of themselves,

---

21   Shakespeare's *Henry IV Part I* and Bridget Boland's 20th-century play *The Prisoner* are examples of dramas that make imaginative sense of unlikely historical events.

and by good poets on account of their actors. For in making show-stopping prize-winning speeches and stretching the story beyond its capacity **1452a** they are often compelled to disrupt the sequence. But since the imitation is not only of a complete action but also of things that produce fear and pity, this comes about most of all when things have happened on account of one another in a paradoxical way. For in this way it is more a source of wonder than if they came from chance or luck, since even among things that come from luck, it is the ones that seem to have happened as if by design that are the most productive of wonder. An instance is the way the statue of Mitys in Argos laid out flat the person responsible for Mitys's death, when it fell on him as he contemplated it, for it seems that such things **10** have not happened randomly; and so necessarily stories of this sort are more beautiful.[22]

Chapter 10

Of stories, some are simple and others complex, for the actions too, of which the stories are imitations, are directly from the start of these sorts. I mean by a simple action one in which, while it comes about as continuous and one in the manner defined,[23] the change takes place without a reversal or discovery; and a complex action is one out of which the change involves a discovery or reversal or both together. And these need to come out of the organization of the story itself, so that they turn out to come to pass **20** out of the things that happened before either out of necessity or by what is likely. For it makes a great difference whether these things here happen on account of these things there or just after them.

---

22 An intrinsic connection between beauty and wonder is described in a famous treatise on beauty by Plotinus (*Ennead* I, treatise 6, section 4). There are two levels in what Aristotle is saying here: a surprising event that is part of a likely sequence is more wondrous than any chance outcome, but even among chance outcomes the most wondrous sort, that have the appearance of design, are more beautiful than random chance outcomes.

23 Continuity of a story was defined first in Ch. 7 as coherence in a likely or necessary sequence; unity in a story was defined in Ch. 8 as coming from the wholeness of one action.

Chapter 11

A reversal is the change to the opposite of the things being done, just as has been said [by others], and this, as we are saying, in accord with what is likely or necessary. For example, in *Oedipus*, one who has come intending to make Oedipus happy and set him free from his fear about his mother, by revealing who he was, does[24] the opposite. And in the *Lynceus*, when one person is being led off to die, while Danaus is following to kill him, it turns out from the things that are done that the latter dies and the former is saved.

And a discovery, **30** as even its name implies, is a change from ignorance to recognition, leading toward either friendship or hostility in people bound for good or bad fortune. A discovery is most beautiful when it happens at the same time as a reversal, as is the case with the one in the *Oedipus*. Now there are also other sorts of discoveries, for it is possible for what was described to happen in relation to nonliving and random things, or to discover whether someone has or has not done something. But the discovery that belongs most to a story and most to an action is the one that was stated. For that sort of discovery and reversal will **1452b** have in it either pity or fear (which are the sorts of actions tragedy was set down as being an imitation of) since being unfortunate and being fortunate will stand side-by-side at such occasions. Now since the discovery is a discovery belonging to certain people, some belong only to one person in relation to the other (when it is clear who one of them is), but sometimes there is need for both of the two to make the discovery; for instance, Iphigeneia is discovered by Orestes by the sending of a letter, but there is a need for another sort of discovery of him by Iphigeneia.[25]

---

24   The words translated "revealing" and "does" are aorists, indicating the suddenness of a reversal. It does not refer to the whole change from happiness to misery that even a simple tragedy would depict. The example is from Sophocles' *Oedipus Tyrannus*, beginning at line 924. (The following example is a lost play from Aristotle's time by Theodectes.)

25   This refers to Euripides' *Iphigeneia among the Taurians*, beginning at line 727.

These, then, are two parts of the story, reversal **10** and discovery, and a third is suffering. Of these, reversal and discovery have been described, and suffering is an action that is destructive or painful, such as deaths in plain view, as well as tortures and woundings and as many other things as are of that sort.

Chapter 12

We spoke before of the parts of tragedy which ought to be treated as forms of it, but these are the separated parts into which it is divided by quantity: prologue, episode, exodus, and choral part, and this last is either the choral entry or a stasimon. These are shared in common by all tragedies, but songs by actors and dirges are peculiar to some. A prologue is the whole portion of the tragedy before the entry **20** of the chorus, an episode is a whole portion of a tragedy that is between whole choral odes, and an exodus is a whole portion of a tragedy after which there is no choral ode. Of the choral part, a choral entry is the first whole vocal performance of the chorus, and a stasimon is a choral ode that is not in an anapestic or trochaic meter,[26] while a dirge is a lamentation shared between the chorus and the actors on stage. We spoke before of the parts of tragedy which ought to be treated as forms of it, but these are the separated parts into which it is divided by quantity.[27]

Chapter 13

What one ought to aim at and what one ought to be on guard against in organizing stories, and where the work proper to tragedy will come from, **30** would be next in order to speak of after the things that have now been said. Now since the putting together of the most beautiful sort of tragedy needs to be not

---

26   These dancing and marching meters would accompany the chorus's entrance or other brief contributions, rather than the extended set-piece of a full choral ode.

27   This odd little chapter, that interrupts the flow of Aristotle's argument about stories, and opens and closes with echoing utterances, seems to imitate a choral interlude.

simple but complex, and this needs to be imitative of things producing fear and pity (since this is the special property of this sort of imitation), it is clear first that decent men ought not to be shown changing from good to bad fortune (since this is neither frightening nor pitiable but repellent) and people of bad character ought not to be shown changing from bad to good fortune (since this is the most untragic thing of all, for it has none of the things a tragedy needs, since it neither arouses love for humanity[28] 1453a nor is it pitiable or frightening); someone of extremely bad character ought not to fall from good to bad fortune either (for while this sort of organization of the story would have a love for humanity in it, it would not have either pity or fear, since one of these has to do with someone's suffering misfortune while not deserving it, the other with his being like us, pity being for a person undeserving of misfortune and fear for one like us, so that the result will be neither pitiable nor frightening). Therefore, what remains is the one between these. This is the sort of person who is not surpassing in virtue and justice, but does not change into misfortune through bad character and vice, but on account of **10** some missing of the mark, if he is among those who are in great repute and good fortune, such as Oedipus and Thyestes and conspicuous men from such families.

It is therefore necessary for the story that is in beautiful shape to be single—not double as some people claim—changing not into good fortune from bad but the opposite way, from good fortune to bad, not through badness of character but on account of a great missing of the mark, either by the sort of person described or by someone better than that rather than worse. What happens is also a sign of this, for at first poets used to recount any random stories, but now the most beautiful tragedies are composed about a few households, for instance **20** about Alcmaeon, Oedipus,

---

28   Love for humanity (*to philanthropon*), here and in Ch. 18, may be a generic feeling that includes both pity (pain at undeserved bad fortune) and righteous indignation (pain at undeserved good fortune), or it may refer only to the latter, a feeling on behalf of humanity in general as opposed to the pity that is felt for someone in particular.

Orestes, Meleager, Thyestes, Telephus, and all the others to whose lot it fell either to suffer or to do terrible things. The most beautiful tragedy that results from the art, then, comes from this sort of organization of the story. For this reason, those who blame Euripides because he does this in his tragedies (and many of his do end in misfortune) are missing the very point. For, as has been said, this is the right thing to do. The greatest sign of this is that, on stage and in competition, such plays show themselves as the most tragic, if they are rightly put on, and Euripides, even if he does not manage other things well, still **30** shows himself to be the most tragic of poets.[29] The second sort of organization of the story is the one said to be first by some people, that has a double organization the way the *Odyssey* does, and ends in opposite ways for the better and worse people. It seems to be first because of a weakness of the spectators, for the poets follow the crowd, making what suits their wishes. But this is not the pleasure that comes from tragedy but one more appropriate to comedy, for there the people most hostile to one another, the way Orestes and Aegisthus are, go away having become friends at the end, and no one is killed by anyone.

Chapter 14

1453b It is possible for what is frightening and pitiable to arise out of the spectacle, but it is also possible for it to arise from the very organization of the actions, and it is exactly this that takes precedence and is the mark of a better poet. For the story ought to be organized in such a way that, even without seeing the actions happening, someone who hears them shudders and feels pity from the way they turn out, the very things one would experience while hearing the story of Oedipus. But to present

---

29   Aristotle criticizes Euripides for his handling of character in *Orestes* and *Iphigeneia in Aulis* (1454a 28-33, 1461b 21), for using unaccountable events in the story in *Medea* (1454a 37-b 2, 1461b 20-21), and for not integrating the chorus into the action in general (1456a 25-27). He is most tragic because of his presentation of terrible suffering (1453a 22, b 39); consider, for example, the lost lines near the end of the *Bacchae* in which, according to many reports, Agave sang a lament over each part in turn of the dismembered body of her son.

this effect through the spectacle is less artful and needs financial resources, while those who, through the spectacle, present not something frightening but only something grotesque **10** have nothing in common with tragedy, for one ought not to seek every sort of pleasure from a tragedy, but the one appropriate to it. And since the poet needs to provide the pleasure that comes from pity and fear by means of an imitation, it is clear that this needs to be embodied in the actions. Let us, then, take up what sorts of things appear terrifying and what sorts arouse compassion when they befall people.

Now it is necessary that such actions belong to people who are, in relation to one another, either friends or enemies or neither. If it is an enemy against an enemy, nothing he is doing or about to do will be pitiable except the suffering in and of itself, nor will it be pitiable when they have neither relation to one another. But when the sufferings come about among friends, **20** such as when a brother kills a brother, or a son a father, or a mother a son, or a son a mother, or one of them is about to do this or some other such thing, these are the situations to be sought. Now it is not open to one to take isolated pieces out of the stories that have come down to us—I mean, say, the killing of Clytemnestra by Orestes or of Eriphyle by Alcmaeon—but the poet ought to make the stories his own and use this heritage in a beautiful way. And let us say more clearly what we mean by "in a beautiful way."

It is possible for the action to happen the way the old poets used to make it happen, with people knowing and recognizing what they were doing, as even Euripides made Medea kill her children. But it is possible **30** to act and yet be ignorant that the action is a terrible deed, and then to discover the kinship afterward, as with Sophocles' Oedipus. (This was in fact outside the drama, but it is put in the tragedy itself in the case of Astydamas's *Alcmaeon* or by Telegonus in *Odysseus Wounded*.) Yet a third possibility besides these is for someone on the point of doing some irreparable harm to discover this before doing it. Besides these there is no other way for things to happen, since it is necessary either to act or not, and either while knowing or not knowing.

The worst thing, worse than these, is to be on the point of acting while recognizing what is involved and not act. It has something repellent about it and is not tragic, since there is no suffering. That is why no one **1454a** makes a story like this, other than in a few details, such as Haemon with Creon in *Antigone*. Second only to this is for such a person to act; it is better for someone ignorant to act, and once having acted to make the discovery, for there is nothing repellent connected with it, and the discovery is awe-striking. But the last possibility is the most powerful[30]; I mean, for example, the way Merope in the *Cresphontes* is on the point of killing her son, and does not kill him but discovers who he is, as the sister discovers her brother in *Iphigeneia*, and the son in the *Helle* discovers his mother when he is on the point of betraying her.

On account of this, as was said long ago, tragedies are **10** not about many families. For in seeking, poets found out not from art but from luck how to present this sort of thing in their stories. So they were compelled to have recourse to these households, the ones that had such sufferings befall them. About the organization of the actions, then, and of what particular sorts the stories ought to be, enough has been said.

Chapter 15

In connection with states of character, there are four things at which one ought to aim. One such thing, and the primary one, is that they be solidly reliable. A state of character will be

---

30 This is usually translated as "best," making it seem to be a direct contradiction of what Aristotle says in the preceding chapter about the most beautiful or most tragic sort of ending. But the superlative here is *kratiston*, with a different root than the comparative in the sentence just before it (*beltion*). Also, the possibility here discussed has a "happy" outcome in a different sense than the double story in which the bad characters end in misfortune and the good ones in good fortune. The *Cresphontes* mentioned next is by Euripides, and the *Iphigeneia* referred to is his *Iphigeneia Among the Taurians*, Chapters 13 and 14 are often viewed as pivoting between two highest examples of tragedy: Sophocles' *Oedipus Tyrannus* and Euripides' *Iphigeneia Among the Taurians*.

present if, as has been said, speech or action makes some choice apparent, whatever it may be, and a solidly reliable choice indicates a solidly reliable character. But this is present **20** in each class of people, for there can be a solidly reliable woman or slave, even though the former of these may perhaps be of lesser character and the latter of a thoroughly low sort. The second thing is that character be fitting; for it is possible for a woman to be manly in character, but it is not fitting for her to be so manly or terrifying. The third thing is that character be lifelike, for this is a different thing from making the character reliable and fitting in the way already described. The fourth thing is that character be consistent, for even if the person showing himself in the imitation is someone who is inconsistent and that sort of character is taken as given, he should still be consistently inconsistent. A model of unnecessary badness of character is, for instance, Menelaus in the *Orestes*; of one **30** that is inappropriate and not fitting, the lament of Odysseus in the *Scylla* or the oration of Melanippe; of an inconsistent one, *Iphigeneia in Aulis*, for when she is begging for her life she is nothing like she is later. And in states of character, just as in the organization of the actions, one should in a similar way always seek either what is necessary or what is likely, namely a person with the sort of character that is either bound or likely to say or do the sorts of things he says or does, as well as that it be necessary or likely for this to happen after that.

It is clear, then, that the resolutions of stories ought to result **1454b** from someone's very character,[31] and not, as in *Medea*, from a mechanical device, or from the things surrounding the

---

31   Most of the manuscripts have the word "story," but there is some textual support for this reading, which makes better sense in this chapter and in itself. The necessary or likely sequence of the story follows an action, the action follows from a choice, and the choice follows from a state of character. This paragraph is Aristotle's only discussion in the *Poetics* of the role of the gods in tragedies; his point is not that their presence makes for bad stories, nor that they are not part of the circumstances of human action, but that the whole of the action that shapes the story, down to its resolution, needs to follow from a choice rooted in a state of character that is consistent, lifelike, and fitting to a decent human being.

running away to the ships in the *Iliad*.[32] Using a mechanical device is something to apply to the things outside the drama, either those that happened before that are impossible for a human being to know, or those later that need foretelling and proclamation, for we grant the gods the ability to see all things. There ought to be nothing unaccountable[33] in the actions, or failing that, it should be outside the tragedy, as with what is in the *Oedipus* of Sophocles.

And since tragedy is an imitation of people better than we are, one ought to imitate good portrait **10** painters, for they too, while rendering the particular form and making likenesses, paint them as more beautiful. So too, the poet, when he imitates people who are quick to anger or lazy or who have other such traits in their characters, ought to make them be decent people who are of those sorts, as Homer made Achilles good and also a model of hardness.[34] So one should be attentive to these things, and in addition to these, to the sensory imagery that necessarily goes along with the poetic art, for it is often possible to miss the mark as a result of it as well. But it has been sufficiently discussed in published writings.[35]

Chapter 16

What a discovery is has been said before, but **20** there are forms of discovery. First is the kind that is least artful and is used most often on account of a lack of resources, that which

---

32 In Euripides' *Medea* (beginning at line 1317), the main character is whisked off the stage on a mechanical crane. In Bk. II of Homer's *Iliad* (beginning at line 110), a chaotic rout is caused by a lying dream and needs the intervention of a goddess to undo the confusion.

33 The word is *alogon*, and some interpreters see this statement as a rejection of the irrational element in human life. But in speaking of fidelity to human character, Aristotle means precisely to make a distinction from fidelity to rational thought and to give the former a higher rank in tragedies. (See 1450b 10-12 and the footnote on it.) In the present context, it is not irrational human choices that are rejected, but unaccountable actions of divine beings; the mysterious motives of Apollo lie behind the action of *Oedipus Tyrannus*, but the drama is wholly shaped by Oedipus's own steadfastness in his choices.

34 See *Iliad* XVI, lines 29-35.

35 It is not clear what writings are meant, but Aristotle discusses this topic quite a bit in the *Rhetoric*, for example in Bk. III, Ch. 11.

takes place through signs. Of these, some are congenital marks, such as "the spear-head that the Earthborn bear" or the stars of the sort Carcinus uses in *Thyestes*; others are acquired, and of these, some are on the body, such as scars, others external, such as necklaces and such as the discovery by means of the canoe in *Tyro*.[36] But it is possible to use even these in either a better or a worse way. For example, Odysseus is discovered by the scar in one way by the nurse and in another way by the swineherds; the instances in which the scar is used for the sake of persuasion are the less artful, as are all things of that sort, but those that come from reversals, **30** as does the one in the washing scene, are better.[37] The second kind are fabricated by the poet, and hence artless. An example is the way Orestes in the *Iphigeneia* induces the discovery that he is Orestes, for while she is discovered by means of the letter, he himself says things that the poet wants but the story does not need; hence it is in a certain way close to the way of missing the mark just mentioned, since it would have been possible for him to bring something. There is also the voice of the shuttle in Sophocles' *Tereus*.[38] The third kind are through memory, by noticing **1455a** something one has seen before, as with the discovery in Dicaeogenes's *Cyprians*, for the one who saw the painting burst into tears, and also in the tale told to Alcinous, for upon hearing the singer playing the lyre, and remembering, Odysseus wept; consequently they were discovered.

The fourth kind are from reasoning, as in the *Libation Bearers*, where Electra reasons that "someone like me has come, but no one is like me except Orestes; therefore he has come." And there is the remark of Polyidus the sophist about the *Iphigeneia*,

---

36   In Astydamus's *Antigone* the descendants of Cadmus have spear-head-shaped birthmarks, and in Carcinus's *Thyestes*, those of Pelops have star-shaped ones. In a lost play of Sophocles, Tyro recognizes the canoe in which she had set adrift her baby sons to save their lives.

37   With the herdsmen, Odysseus tells them who he is, and points to his scar to persuade them, but with the nurse, he is discovered when she washes his feet (*Odyssey* XXI, 205 and following, and XIX, 386 and following).

38   A woman whose tongue had been cut out wove a picture of her attacker on a loom.

for he says it is likely Orestes would have reasoned that his sister was sacrificed and he would end up being sacrificed too.[39] And in Theodectes' *Tydeus*, the one who has come to find his son reasons that he himself **10** is lost. And there is the instance in the *Phineidai*: on seeing the place, people reason out their lot, that it was their allotted portion to die in that place since they had also been abandoned there. There is also a kind of discovery put together out of the misreasoning of the audience, as in *Odysseus the False Messenger*, for an assumption fabricated by the poet that, since he and no other could bend the bow, then if he says he could recognize the bow (which he had not seen), through this [his recognizing the bow] he would be discovered on account of that [his ability to bend it] makes a faulty inference.[40]

But the best discovery of all is the kind that arises out of the actions themselves, so that the awe-striking impact comes about from things that are likely, as in the *Oedipus* of Sophocles and the *Iphigeneia* (for it is likely that one would want to send a letter).[41] It is only discoveries of these sorts **20** that are without contrived signs and external ornaments.[42] Second best are those that come from reasoning.

Chapter 17

In order to organize the stories and work them out with their wording, one ought, as much as possible, to put them before the eyes.[43] For one who sees things most vividly in this way, as if he were among the very actions taking place, would find what

---

39   How this would lead to his being discovered emerges in the next chapter.

40   The play is not known, the manuscripts are uncertain in these lines, and Aristotle's grammar here is unclear, but the general sense seems to be that one who could recognize the bow was not necessarily the one who could bend and string it. Whether the poet was intentionally inviting an erroneous conclusion or unintentionally falling into one is not clear either. An example of the former sort is given at 1460a 18-26.

41   Euripides, *Iphigeneia Among the Taurians*, beginning at line 578.

42   Literally necklaces, which may be a metaphor for the way contrived signs are strung around the outside of the story as well as a typical example of one.

43   Aristotle gives examples of wording that fail or succeed in this respect in the *Rhetoric*, at the beginning of Bk. III, Ch. 11.

is appropriate and would least overlook incongruities. A sign of this is what Carcinus was blamed for, because he brought Amphiaraus back out of the shrine, which he overlooked by not visualizing it; on the stage it fell flat because the audience was scornful of this. As many things as possible ought also to be **30** worked out with gestures, for those who are immersed in the experiences are the most persuasive from nature itself, and one who is undergoing a storm of distress produces a storm of distress most truthfully, as one who is in a fit of temper produces anger. Hence, the poetic art belongs either to a naturally gifted person or an insane one, since those of the former sort are easily adaptable and the latter are out of their senses.

The plots, both those that have been made **1455b** and those the poet makes up himself, ought to be laid out in a general way and then in that manner be given episodes and be filled out. I mean that one could contemplate the general content of, say, the *Iphigeneia* in this way: a certain girl has been offered for sacrifice and has vanished in an obscure manner from her sacrificers, and come to be settled in another land in which it was a custom to sacrifice foreigners to the goddess; she came to hold this priestly office, and at a later time it turned out that the brother of this priestess came (and the fact that the god decreed that he go there and for what purpose is outside the story); but having come and having been captured, when he is on the point of being sacrificed he induces his discovery, either in Euripides' way **10** or as Polyidus made it up, by his making the likely remark that, after all, not only his sister but also he himself had to be sacrificed—and his rescue came from that. After these things, as soon as the names have been put in, one ought to give it episodes, but in such a way that the episodes are appropriate, such as the madness in Orestes through which he is captured and his rescue by way of the ritual cleansing.

Now in dramas the episodes are brief, but epic poetry gets its length from them. For the plot of the *Odyssey* is not long: a certain man, away from home for many years and closely watched by Poseidon, is alone; and further, things at home are such that his property **20** is being used up by suitors and his son plotted against; he himself, having endured storms, arrives, and once he has let some people discover who he is, having made an attack, he comes through safely and destroys his enemies. This, then, is what is its very own, and everything else is episodes.

Chapter 18

There is in every tragedy a build-up and a resolution,[44] the things outside the drama and often some of those inside it being the build-up, and the rest the resolution. I speak of what is from the beginning up to that part which is the last one out of which there is a change into good or bad fortune a building-up, and what is from the beginning of the change up to the end a resolving. In this sense, in the *Lynceus* of Theodectes **30** the prior actions, the capture of the child, and their own capture in turn are a building-up, and the part from the accusation of murder up to the end is a resolving.

And the forms of tragedy are four (since the parts that have been singled out are also that many): the complex tragedy, the whole [plot] of which consists of reversal and discovery; the tragedy of suffering, such as **1456a** the ones about Ajax or Ixion; the tragedy of character, such as *The Phthian Women* and the *Peleus*; and the fourth is the [simple spectacle],[45] such as *The Daughters of Phorcis*, the *Prometheus*, and the ones set in Hades. Above all, then, one ought to try to include them all, or if not, the greatest ones and the greatest number, especially since people are now in the habit of running the poets down. Since there have been poets who were good at each part taken one at a time, people demand that one person surpass what was good in every one in particular.

---

44 Literally a tying and an untying.

45 The manuscripts have either a void space where the name of the fourth kind would be, or a few letters that do not make a word. The letters could look a little like the word for spectacle, but the list is referred to at the beginning of Ch. 24 with the fourth kind called simple.

But it is not as just to say tragedies are different or the same on any basis other than the story, and this means considering those of which the complexity[46] and resolution are the same. And many poets who are good at complicating **10** are bad at resolving, but one ought to weld them both together just right.

And one should remember the thing that has often been said, and not give a tragedy an organization suited for epic poetry; by what is suited for epic poetry I mean a multiple story, as if one were to make the whole story of the *Iliad* into a tragedy. For there, on account of its length, its parts take on an appropriate magnitude, but for a conception suited to dramas it much oversteps the bounds. A sign of this is that all those who make a tragedy of the whole sacking of Troy, and not part by part as Euripides did, or of the whole Niobe story, and not as Aeschylus treated it, either fall flat or come out badly in competition, since even Agathon fell into failure in this way alone.

But in reversals and **20** simple actions as well, poets hit the mark they want to hit wonderfully well, since this is to depict something with tragic suffering that arouses love for humanity. And this occurs when someone of theoretical wisdom but with a bad character, like Sisyphus, is tricked, or a brave but unjust man is beaten in a fight.[47] And this is even likely in the sense in which Agathon speaks of it, since it is likely that many things happen contrary to what is likely.

And the chorus ought to be conceived as one of the actors and part of the whole, sharing in the action, not as in Euripides

---

46   A noun encompassing the reversals and discoveries of a complex tragedy is here used where Aristotle before spoke of the build-up present in every tragedy.

47   These cases of "poetic justice" concern characters who get what they deserve, and hence, by the standard described in Ch. 13, would arouse not pity but righteous indignation. The examples given also seem to involve people who have superior qualities, on whose behalf we would not feel fear. Since the effect the poets like to achieve with them needs no reversals (being achievable in simple stories) and the outcome stands likelihood on its head, such plays seem not to be tragedies in any genuine sense at all, but a self-indulgence of the poets that audiences like. For this reason, the word *tragikon* in the previous sentence is translated (as it is explained at 1453b 39) as "with tragic suffering." This paragraph is the only reference in the *Poetics* to "flawed" characters.

but as in Sophocles. In the rest of the poets, the odes are no more part of the story than of some other tragedy; that is why they sing interludes, Agathon having been the one who first **30** started such a thing. And yet how would it differ from singing interludes if one were to fit in a speech from one play into another, or even a whole episode?

Chapter 19

There has been discussion about the other forms, then, but what remains is to speak about wording and thinking. Now let the things concerned with thinking be the ones set down in the writings on rhetoric, since this belongs more particularly to that pursuit.[48] And the things that have to do with thinking are all those that need to be presented by the agency of speech. Parts within these are demonstrating, refuting, and the presenting of passions (such as **1456b** pity, fear, anger, and everything of that sort), and also magnifying and minimizing. And it is clear that in the actions as well one needs to use things that have the same look as these, whenever pitiable or terrifying or great or likely things need to be presented; they differs, though, to this extent, that the latter need to be apparent without explanation, while the former are presented in the speech by the speaker and come about on account of the speech. For what would the task of the speaker be if things were to appear in the way they needed to and not through the speech?

Of the things having to do with wording, one form of study concerns the modes of speaking, **10** which it belongs to the actor's art to know, as well as to someone who has the master art for this sort of thing,[49] such topics as what a command is, and what a prayer, a narration, a threat, a question, an answer,

---

48   Much of Aristotle's *Rhetoric*, especially Bk. II, Chs. 18-26, deals with the kinds of arguments and evidence that are suited to public use rather than to the most precise studies.

49   Perhaps rhetoric, which studies the same things for use in the legislative assembly, the courtroom, and public ceremonies, or, another step higher, the branch of logic (which Aristotle calls the analytic art) pursued in *On Interpretation*.

and any other such thing there may be are. For on account of knowing or being ignorant of these things, no blame whatever worthy of serious notice carries over to the poetic art. For how could anyone suppose that what Protagoras blamed Homer for was a missing of the mark, that thinking he was making a prayer he gave a command in saying "Sing, goddess, of the wrath"? For he says that to bid someone to do or not do something is a command. Therefore, let this be passed over as being a study belonging to another art and not to poetics.

Chapter 20

20 The parts of all wording are these: letter, syllable, connecting word, noun, verb, joint-word, inflection, and phrase. Now a letter is an indivisible vocal sound, though not every such sound, but one out of which a composite sound naturally comes about (since there are also indivisible sounds belonging to animals, none of which I call a letter). They are partitioned into vowels, semi-vocal consonants, and mute consonants. Those that have an audible sound without contact [in the mouth] are vowels, and those that have an audible sound with such contact, such as S and R, are semi-vocal consonants, but no mute consonant has a sound by itself with such contact, but along with **30** the ones that have some sound it becomes audible, such as G and D. These differ by the shaping of the mouth and the places of contact, by rough and smooth breathing, by long and short duration, and also by acute, grave, and in-between pitch; what concerns them each by each is appropriate to study in writings about the art of meter. A syllable is a sound without meaning, composed of a mute consonant and a letter having a sound, for GR is a syllable without an A as well as GRA with the A. But to study the differences among these also belongs to the art of meter.

A connecting word is a sound without meaning which **1457a** neither hinders nor produces a single sound with meaning composed naturally out of a number of sounds, and which is

at the ends or in the middle of such composites, but does not
fit when placed by itself at the beginning of a phrase; examples
are *men*, *êtoi*, and *de*. Or it is a sound without meaning which,
out of a number of sounds with meaning, naturally produces
one sound with meaning. A joint-word is a sound without
meaning which shows the beginning or end of a phrase or a
division of one, such as *amphi*, *peri*, and the rest. Or it is a sound
without meaning which neither hinders nor produces a single
sound with meaning composed naturally out of a number of
sounds, and **10** which is at the ends or in the middle of such
composites.[50]

A noun is a composite sound with meaning, not indicating
time, of which no part is meaningful in itself; for in a double
noun we do not use each part as carrying meaning in the way it
does by itself, as in Theodore, "dore" has no meaning.[51] A verb is
a composite sound with meaning, indicating time, of which no
part has meaning by itself, as in the case of nouns. For "human-
being" and "white-thing"[52] do not indicate at what time, but
"marches" and "marched" carry the additional meanings of the
present time and the past.

An inflection belongs to a noun or a verb, carrying a
meaning in one way as either of or to this **20** or as many such
cases as there are, or as one or many, as with "human beings"
or "human being," and in another way in accord with the things
that pertain to an actor's intonation, as according to a question
or command—"Marched?" or "March!" is an inflecting of a
verb in these forms.

---

50   The connecting word corresponds to both particles and conjunctions, while the joint-
     word corresponds to both prepositions and articles. They are all without meaning in the
     same way that mute consonants are without sound: they contribute to the meaning of a
     composite whole without being able to carry any meaning by themselves.

51   The phrase *theou dôron* (god's gift) combines meaningful parts into a composite
     meaning, but in the name *Theodôros* the parts are heard differently, not as forms of the
     words they are derived from.

52   The hyphens here reflect the fact that both Greek examples are single words. The first
     is a noun with no exact one-word equivalent in English and the second is an adjective
     used as a substantive.

But a phrase is a composite sound with meaning of which some parts mean something by themselves. For not every phrase is put together out of nouns and verbs, but it is possible for there to be a phrase without verbs, such as the definition of a human being, though it will always have a part that means something, like the "Cleon" in "Cleon is marching." And a phrase is one in two ways, for it is either what means one thing, or what comes from connecting a number of things; for instance, the *Iliad* **30** is one by connection, but the definition of a human being by meaning one thing.[53]

Chapter 21

The forms of word are simple and double, and by simple I mean one such as "earth" which is not put together out of things having meaning. Of the double form, one sort is made of a part with meaning and a part without (except that within the word, it is not made of one part with meaning and one without), while another sort is put together out of things with meaning; and a word could be triple or quadruple or many-fold, as are many words used by the Massalians, such as Hermocaicoxanthus.[54] **1457b** And every word is either prevalent, foreign, a metaphor, embellished,[55] made up, lengthened, shortened, or altered. I call prevalent what everybody in a group uses, and foreign what is used by another group, so that it is obvious that the same word is capable of being both foreign and prevalent, though not to the

---

53   The word translated "phrase" is *logos*. Its meaning in this chapter extends beyond phrases to sentences and finally to the *Iliad*, all of which are hierarchical wholes with meanings subordinated to an overarching unity of meaning. A phrase is its minimum instance. A word that comes close to spanning all its instances in this passage might be discourse.

54   A word formed from the names of three rivers. The place this tribe inhabited is now Marseilles. The manuscripts have a gap where there were presumably other examples of their multiple words. A 20th century example would be the German word for reparations, which is literally again-good-making.

55   No explanation or example of an embellished word (*kosmos*) is given in the *Poetics*, but in the *Rhetoric* (III, 2) Aristotle speaks of embellishment as using the name of a better species of the same genus, such as calling begging praying, or simply as choosing a more beautiful synonym, such as rosy-fingered instead of purple-fingered or red-fingered.

same people, since to the Cypriots *sigunon* (spear) is prevalent, but to us it is foreign.

A metaphor is a carrying over of a word belonging to something else, from genus to species, from species to genus, from species to species, or by analogy. By from genus **10** to species, I mean, for instance "here stands my ship" (for being tied to a mooring is a sort of standing); by from species to genus "truly ten thousand good things has Odysseus done" (for ten thousand is a many which here is used in place of "many"); by from species to species, for instance "drawing off the soul with bronze" and "cutting [water] with indestructible bronze" (for here drawing has conveyed cutting and cutting drawing, since both are sorts of taking away).[56] And I speak of analogy whenever a second thing has to a first a relation similar to that which a fourth has to a third; for one will state the fourth in place of the second or the second in place of the fourth, and sometimes people add **20** the thing to which the replaced word is related. I mean, for instance, a drinking-bowl has to Dionysus a similar relation to that of a shield to Ares; accordingly, one will call the drinking-bowl a shield of Dionysus and the shield a drinking-bowl of Ares. Or old age is to life as evening is to a day; accordingly, one will call evening the old age of day, or, as Empedocles does, call old age the evening of life, or the sunset of life. For some of the things said by analogy there is no word laid down, but it will be stated in a similar way nonetheless. For example, to scatter seed is to sow, but there is no word for scattering flame from the sun; but this has to the sun a relation similar to that of sowing to seed, and hence "sowing the god-created **30** flame" is said. And it is also possible to use a metaphor made in this manner in another way, calling something by the borrowed name but negating one of the things proper to it, if,

56 Both lines are from Empedocles' *Purifications*, where a bronze knife cuts the life from a sacrificial animal and a bronze vessel draws water from five springs for ritual cleansing. The original of the second has been used to supply the direct object, and to give a preference to a manuscript variant for the adjective.

for instance, one were to speak of a shield not as a drinking-bowl of Ares but as a wineless drinking-bowl.

A made-up word is one that the poet himself sets down for something not called that by anyone at all, for there seem to be some words of this sort, such as "sprouters" for horns and "pray-er" for a priest. A word is lengthened **1458a** or shortened if, in the one case a vowel longer than the proper one or an inserted syllable is used, and in the other case something is taken away from it; for example, *poleôs* is lengthened to *polêos* and *Pêleidou* to *Pêlêiadeô*, while instances of shortened words are *kri*, *dô*, and "one *ops* comes from the pair."[57] A word is altered whenever one leaves part of the word people use and makes up part of it, such as "on the rightward breast" in place of "right."

Of nouns[58] themselves, some are masculine, some feminine, and some in-between; all those that end in nu, rho, or sigma, **10** or those letters that are compounds of sigma (and these are two, psi and ksi) are masculine, while all those that end in one of the vowels that are always long, which are eta and omega, or in one of the lengthened vowels, alpha, are feminine. So it turns out that the letters in which the masculines and feminines end are equal in number, since psi and ksi are compounded [sigmas]. No noun ends in a mute consonant or a short vowel, and only three end in iota—*meli* (honey), *kommi* (gum), and *peperi* (pepper)—and five in upsilon. And the in-between nouns end in these as well as in nu and sigma.

Chapter 22

The virtue of wording is to be clear and not flat. Now the clearest wording consists of prevalent words, but it is **20** flat; the poetry of Cleophon and that of Sthenelus are models of

---

57   The lengthened examples are genitives of the words for city and son of Peleus; the shortened ones are from *krithê* (barley), *dôma* (house), and *opsis* (sight).

58   In the preceding chapter, *onoma* was translated as "noun," but in most of this chapter as "word." This last paragraph refers only to nouns in the nominative singular, and even so has many exceptions, though much of it is accurate for proper names (another meaning of *onoma*).

this. But the use of unfamiliar words lends dignity and departs from the local idiom; by unfamiliar I mean foreign, metaphoric, lengthened, and everything besides what is prevalent. But if one makes all the words of these sorts, there will be either a riddle or a barbarism, a riddle when something is all made of metaphors and a barbarism when it is all made of foreign words. For that which speaks of its subjects in words a hearer is incapable of connecting with them has the look of a riddle. Now by putting together other words it is not possible to produce this result, but with metaphors it is possible, as in "I saw a man glue bronze **30** on a man with fire"[59] and things like that. But things made all of foreign words are barbarisms. Therefore there ought to be a blending of these in some manner, since what is not of the local idiom, such as a foreign word, a metaphor, an embellished word, or a word of the other forms mentioned, will keep the wording from being flat, while the prevalent words will produce clarity.

Not the least part of what **1458b** contributes to what is clear and non-idiomatic in wording are the lengthenings, shortenings, and alterings of words, for by being different from what is prevalent and going outside what is customary, they will produce something not of the local idiom, but by their having some share in what is customary, there will be something clear. So those who find fault with this way of talking and make fun of the poet, as the old Eucleides did, are not right in blaming him on the grounds that it is easy to make poetry if one is going to be given license to lengthen words as much as he wants; he made a parody in this very sort of wording: "I saw Epichares marching to Marathon"[60] **10** Now making it obvious in some way that one is using this manner of wording is funny, but measure is needed

---

59   A medical procedure called cupping involved placing a heated bronze bowl over a small incision, to draw out blood as the instrument cooled.

60   Two short vowels in Eucleides' Greek have to be sounded as long to make the line scan in dactylic hexameter. A little artificiality in the stress accents gives a similar effect in the translation. A second example is given, but the manuscript readings are incomplete and vary widely.

for all parts of the art in common; for one who used metaphors, foreign words, and the other forms of wording inappropriately on purpose for laughs would get the same effect. How much difference what is fitting makes in epic verses may be observed if one inserts words into the meter. And if in the case of a foreign word, or metaphors, or the other forms, one were to substitute prevalent words, one would see that what we are saying is true.

For example, the same iambic line was made **20** by Aeschylus and Euripides with only one word replaced, a foreign one in place of a customary prevalent one, and while one appears beautiful, the other is of a dime-a-dozen sort. For Aeschylus in his *Philoctetes* made the line "The cancer that eats the flesh of my foot" but the other poet, in place of "eats" substituted "feasts on." Or consider "Now against me, you who are little, a nobody, and unimpressive,"[61] if one were to say it, substituting prevalent words, as "Now against me, you who are short, weak, and ugly," Or "He set down a plain stool and a little table" **30** if it were "He set down a crummy stool and a short table," or "the seashore is roaring" if it were "the seashore is yelling." Ariphrades too made fun of the tragic poets because they use these things that no one would say in conversation, such as "from the house far" and not "far from the house," or "thine" or "and I thee…"[62] or **1459a** "Achilles concerning" and not "concerning Achilles," and all that sort of thing. For by not being in prevalent words, all such things produce what is not of the local idiom in its wording, but he was ignorant of this.

But while it is a great thing to use each of the forms mentioned in an appropriate way, as well as double and foreign words, much the greatest form of wording is the metaphorical. For this alone can not be grasped from anyone else and is a sign of natural gifts, since to use metaphors well is to have insight into what is alike. Among the words, the double ones are

---

61   The Cyclops to Odysseus at *Odyssey* IX, 515. The next example is *Odyssey* XX, 259.

62   The second archaic pronoun is actually in the third person.

especially suited to dithyrambs, the foreign ones **10** to heroic verse, and the metaphorical ones to iambic verse. In heroic verse, all the forms mentioned are useful, but in iambic verse, since it imitates talking as much as possible, all those words one might use in talk are fitting, and words of that sort are prevalent ones, metaphors, and embellished ones.

About tragedy, then, and the imitation that takes place in action, let what has been said be sufficient for us.

Chapter 23

About the art of narrative imitation in meter, it is clear that one ought to organize the stories just as in tragedies, as dramatic, concerned with one action, whole and complete, having **20** a beginning, middle, and end, in order that they might, like one whole living thing, produce the appropriate sort of pleasure; the putting together of them ought not to be made like that of histories, in which it is necessary that they make a display not of one action but of one time, with all the things that happened in that time involving one or more people, each of the events related to the others in any random way. For just as the sea battle at Salamis and the battle with the Carthaginians in Sicily happened at the same time, while in no way converging to the same end, so too things can sometimes happen one after the other in successive times from which there comes no one end. But well nigh the majority of poets do **30** this. Hence, as we said already, in this respect too Homer would appear next to the others like the voice of a god, in not even attempting to make a poem out of the war as a whole, even though it had a beginning and an end. For the story would have had to be too long, and not easily taken in all at once, or if he had moderated it in length, it would have become complicated in its variety. But as it is, he selected one part, and made use of episodes from many others, such as the catalogue of ships, and he divides up his poem with other episodes. But the rest of the poets make poems about one person **1459b** or one time or one action with many parts, as did those who made the *Cypria* and the *Little Iliad*.[63] So for this very reason, while only one or two tragedies each are made from the *Iliad* and *Odyssey*, many are made from the *Cypria* and more than eight from the *Little Iliad*, namely *The Judgment of Arms, Philoctetes, Neoptolemus, Eurypylus, The Begging, The Laconian Women, The Sack of Troy, The Sailing Home*, as well as *Sinon* and *The Trojan Women*.

Chapter 24

Also, epic poetry ought to have the same forms as tragedy, since it too is either simple or complex, inclining toward character or suffering. And its **10** parts are the same, outside of song-making and spectacle, for as well as needing its thinking and wording to be done beautifully, it also needs reversals, discoveries, and suffering, all of which Homer was the first to use, and used in an accomplished way. Each of his poems has an organization, the *Iliad* as a simple story of suffering, the *Odyssey* a story of character that is complex (for it is discovery through and through). And adding to these things, he surpassed everyone in wording and thinking.

But as against its organization, epic poetry differs from tragedy in its length and its meter. Now of its length, the limit mentioned is sufficient, since the beginning and end need to be capable of being taken in view **20** together. This would be possible if their organizations were shorter than the ancient epics but came up to the length of the number of tragedies given at one hearing. But epic poetry has something peculiar to it that tends toward its being extended to a great length, since in tragedy it is not possible to imitate many parts of the action going on at the same time, but only the part of it on the stage and involving the actors. But in epic poetry, since it is narration, it is possible to make many parts be accomplished together, by which means, when they are appropriate, the bulk of the poem

---

63   Respectively, a "prequel" to the *Iliad*, beginning with the judgment of Paris, and a sequel, beginning with the contest for Achilles' armor.

is increased in such a way that this is good for magnificence as well as for giving the hearer **30** changes and bringing in dissimilar episodes. For quickly giving people their fill of what is similar makes tragedies fall flat.

And the heroic meter has been fitted to it by experience. For if anyone were to make a narrative imitation in any other meter, or in a combination of many, the inappropriateness of it would be obvious. For the heroic is the most stately and weighty of the meters (which is why it also admits most of all of foreign words and metaphors, since narrative imitation is also out of the ordinary in relation to the other forms), while the iambic and the [trochaic] tetrameter meters **1460a** are suited to motion, the latter to dancing and the former to acting. And it would be still more out of place if one were to mix them, as Chaeremon did. Hence no one has made a long organized poem in any meter other than the heroic, but as we said, nature itself teaches one to choose what is fitting to it.

And Homer is worthy to be praised for many other things, but especially because he alone among the poets is not ignorant of what he himself needs to do. For the poet himself ought to speak the least, since it is not by this that he is an imitator. The other poets themselves take the leading part throughout the whole, and imitate few things and on few occasions, but Homer, after **10** a short prologue, immediately brings in a man or a woman or some other character,[64] and none of them is depicted without character but as having a character.

Now while a source of wonder needs to be produced in tragedies, there is more room in epic poetry, since we are not looking at the person acting, for something unaccountable,[65] by

---

64 That is, a god or a goddess. This rare use of *êthos* for a person rather than a state of character helps hammer home the point: Homer's human beings and gods are all fully realized, never place-holders in a narrative in which the narrator takes center stage.

65 As at 1454b 6, the word is *alogon*. There it referred to disruptions of the consequences of human actions by divine interventions. Here is refers to any violations of inherent likelihood or likely sequence. In neither place does it have any reference to the irrational side of human life, or to our illogical beliefs, which, in this very paragraph, Aristotle recommends that the poet make use of.

means of which a source of wonder results most easily. For the circumstances of the chasing of Hector would appear ludicrous if they were on a stage, with some people standing there and not chasing him while one person warns them off with a headshake, but in the epic verses [the absurdity] goes unnoticed.[66] And wonder is pleasant; a sign of this is the way everybody tells news by adding things to it, so as to give delight. But it is Homer most of all who has taught everyone else how they ought to say things that are false. **20** This involves misreasoning. For people believe that whenever, this being so, that is so, or this coming to be so, that comes to be so, then if the latter is the case, the former will be or become so too; but this is false. Hence, whenever there is a first false thing, but when it is the case it is necessary that another thing be or become true, one ought to add that other thing; for by knowing that latter thing to be true, our soul misreasons that the first thing is true too. A model of this is what happens in the washing scene.[67]

So one ought to take likely but impossible things[68] in preference to possible but unbelievable things, and not to organize plots out of unaccountable parts; the most preferable thing is for plots to have nothing unaccountable in them, or failing that, to have them outside what is made into the story, like **30** Oedipus's not knowing how Laius was killed, and not in the drama, like people's telling about the Pythian Games in *Electra*[69] or the non-speaking person who comes to Mysia from Tegea in the *Mysians*. So to say that the story would be ruined is ridiculous, since one ought not to organize stories in such a

---

66   Homer describes the scene as taking place "as in a dream" (*Iliad* XXII, 199-207).

67   That is, in Bk. XIX of the *Odyssey*. Penelope tests the lying story the disguised Odysseus tells about who he is, and he proves it by describing details that would be known only to someone who had knowledge of Odysseus, whom he claimed to have met.

68   An impossible thing can be a likely consequence of some other false thing, or, by the technique explained in the preceding paragraph, be given an illusion of likelihood by the use of true things that would be consequences of it.

69   An anachronism in Sophocles' version; he is probably the author of the next example also, from a lost play comedians made fun of.

way in the first place. But if one does put in such a thing, and it appears to be possible to treat it in a more reasonable way, that too is absurd, since even in the *Odyssey* it should become obvious that the unaccountable things having to do with his being put ashore[70] would not be **1460b** tolerated if a low-grade poet had made them. But as it is, Homer hides the absurdity by making it pleasant with the other things that are good. But it is in the parts without action[71] that one ought to work things up laboriously in the wording, and not in parts that display character or thinking, since wording that is too brilliant pushes character and thinking back into obscurity.

Chapter 25

As for problems and solutions, how many forms they come out of and of what sorts they are would become evident to those who contemplate them in this way: since the poet is an imitator, just exactly as if he were a painter or some other sort of maker of images, it is necessary that he always imitate some one among things **10** that are three in number, either what sort something was or is, or what sort people say it is and it seems to be, or what sort it ought to be. And these things are delivered in wording in which there are foreign words and metaphors and many modifications of the wording, for we grant these sorts of license to poets. And in addition to these things, there is not the same sort of correctness in the poetic art as in the political art, nor is it the same in any other art as it is in poetics. But a twofold way of missing the mark belongs to the poetic art itself, one belonging to it in itself, the other incidental to it. For if the

---

70 Book XIII, beginning at line 114, where Odysseus stays asleep while the ship he is on runs aground in Ithaca, he is carried ashore in his bedding, and the Phaeacians' many gifts are piled beside him.

71 Aristotle may be referring to the choral odes, but another common feature of many tragedies is the speech given by a messenger, whose character and thinking may be of no interest, where the poet can let his skill with words become prominent. Shakespeare's *Richard II* is a later example of a play that is marred by too much indulgence in clever wordplay not always suited to or distinguished among the characters.

poet was incapable of imitating what he chose to imitate,[72] the missing of the mark is within the art itself, but if the choosing was not done correctly, but described a horse with both right legs swung forward, the missing of the mark was in relation to a particular art **20** such as medicine or any other art whatsoever, and not in relation to his own art. So one ought to resolve the criticisms in the problems by examining them from these standpoints.

First, there are criticisms directed to the art itself: he has made impossible things; he has missed the mark. But this is the right thing to do if one hits the mark that is end at which the art itself aims (for the end has been stated)[73] that is, if in this way one makes that thing itself or some other part of the poem more awe-striking. A model is the chasing of Hector. If, however, the end also admits of being present in accord with the art that concerns these things, either more so or not less so, then it was not the right thing to do, for one ought, if possible, to miss the mark in no way at all.

Also, to which of the two does **30** the missing of the mark belong, the things resulting from the art or from another incidental one? For it is a lesser thing if one does not know that a female deer has no horns than if one depicts her without capturing the image. But if on top of this the criticism is made that the imitation is not true, perhaps it is instead as it ought to be; for instance, Sophocles too said that he made people of the sort they ought to be, while Euripides made them of the sort they are, and the criticism is to be resolved in this way. But if it is resolved in neither of the two ways, it might be that people say it's that way, for perhaps it is not better to say it that way, and not

---

72   The manuscripts have a gap in this clause; instead of following the insertions made by editors, the translation rearranges the syntax of the words that are present.

73   The end of the poetic art, in tragedy and epics at least, was identified in the last chapter with producing wonder. Wonder was spoken of first at 1452a 4 for the effect of a paradoxical outcome that comes about by a likely sequence. Twice, forms of the word awe-striking (*ekplēktikon*) have been used in connection with discoveries (1454a 4, 1455a 17).

true either, but, if it so happens, **1461a** it's just as Xenophanes claims,[74] then still, people do say it. And some things perhaps, while not better, still used to be that way, as in what has to do with the weapons, "their spears upright on heel-spikes"[75] since they were accustomed to leave them that way at the time, just as the Illyrians do even now. And as to whether something has been said or done by someone in a beautiful way or not, one must examine it not only by looking to the thing itself that is done or said to see if it is of serious moral stature or of a low sort, but also by looking to the person who is doing or saying it, and to whom, or when, or for whom, or for the sake of what end (such as for a greater good, that it might come about, or on account of a greater evil, that it might be fended off).

But some things one **10** needs to resolve by looking to the wording, for instance that "first [Apollo's plague attacked] the mules" uses a foreign word, for perhaps it does not mean mules, but guards.[76] And with Dolon, "he was certainly badly formed" means not that his body was out of proportion but that his face was ugly, since the Cretans call a good-looking face a good-looking form.[77] And "mix the drink livelier" means not undiluted, as for a drunkard, but more quickly. Another sort is said by a metaphor, as in "all the gods and men slept through the night" while at the same time, he says, "then he would gaze into the Trojan plain, with its din of flutes and pipes," for "all" is said in place of "many" by a **20** metaphor, since an all is a certain sort of many.[78] And there is "she alone has no part [in the baths

---

74   He blamed Homer and Hesiod for depicting gods in human form, and full of human vices.

75   *Iliad* X, 152-3.

76   That is, perhaps the word *ourêas* in *Iliad* I, 50 is a dialect variation not of the word for mule, with a lengthened first syllable, but of the word for guard, with an inserted second and altered third syllable. The guards would be posted on the outlying areas of the camp.

77   The critics' quibble with *Iliad* X, 316 was that Dolon was called a fast runner, but also called deformed. The next example is from IX, 202.

78   *Iliad* X, 1-2, 11, 13. The first part is slightly misquoted, with a piece of II, 1 substituted, but in fact the word "all" is not in either place, though it is implied in both in the word *alloi*, "[all] the rest of them."

of Ocean]," since by a metaphor the best known instance is the only one.[79] And the way Hippias the Thasian resolved "we grant it to him to satisfy his prayer" and "which is rotted by the rain" is by tone of voice.[80] Others are resolved by being divided, such as Empedocles' "Soon they grew mortal which before had learned to be immortal, and the pure before were mixed."[81] Others by an ambiguity—"the night is fully/more than two parts gone"— for the word *pleiô* is ambiguous. Others by a habit of speaking; people say the mixture [of wine and water] is wine, and hence is produced "a shin-guard of newly worked tin" and they call iron-workers bronze-smiths, and hence **30** Ganymede is said to pour wine for Zeus, though the gods do not drink wine. But this last one might be said by a metaphor.[82]

And whenever any word seems to imply any contradiction, one ought to examine in how many ways this might be meant in what is said; for example, in "by it the bronze spear was held back," one ought to examine in how many ways it is possible to be hindered by this,[83] in this or that particular way, so that one might conceive it in the most suitable way. This is directly opposite to **1461b** the way Glaucon says that some people without any reason preconceive something, and once they have given it a verdict of guilty they reason from it and, as though whatever seems to them is what has been said, lay the blame on

---

79   The Great Bear (or big dipper) is not the only constellation that never sets even partially, as *Iliad* XVIII, 489 seems to say.

80   A change of accent in the first makes the verb imperative, and a change of breathing in the second makes it "not rotted by the rain." Both are from the *Iliad* again, but the first is an ancient variant of II, 15 not in our texts, and our texts of the second (XXIII, 328) incorporate Hippias's version.

81   Were the pure-before mixed, or were the pure before-mixed? The subject is the four elements.

82   The night that is two-thirds or more gone (i.e., beginning or well into the third and last watch) is from *Iliad* X, 252, the shin-guard (or greave) is said to be of tin (the more important part of its alloy?) at XXI, 592, and Ganymede's nectar-pouring function is named by its human analogue at XX, 234.

83   At *Iliad* XX, 272, Aeneas's spear penetrates into Achilles' shield, but is held back at or by the gold layer, which would be expected to be on the outside, but perhaps it pierces the layer that keeps it from going all the way through.

the poet if anything is contradictory to their own supposition. And this is what has happened with the things having to do with Icarius, for people suppose that he is Laconian, and then it is absurd that Telemachus does not meet up with him when he goes to Sparta.[84] But perhaps it is the way the Cephallenians say, for they claim that Odysseus married from among their people, and that the name was Icadius and not Icarius; and it is likely that the problem is due to a mistake.

On the whole, something impossible ought to be **10** traced back to the poetry, to what is better, or to an opinion. With a view to the poetry, an impossible thing that is believable is preferable to an unbelievable thing that is possible. And those whom Zeuxis used to paint are of that former sort, but that is better, for one ought to improve on one's model. Unaccountable things ought to be traced back to what people say, and in this way it is even possible that then they are no longer unaccountable, since it is likely even for something contrary to what is likely to happen.[85] One ought to look at things said in a contradictory way just as refutations in arguments are looked at, to see whether the same thing is being taken, and in the same relation and the same manner, and how it stands either in relation to what the poet himself says or what a sensible person assumes. But there is a right sort of blame, both for unaccountability and for viciousness, whenever, without there **20** being any necessity for it, one uses something unaccountable, as Euripides uses Aegeus,[86] or uses some badness of character, such as that of Menelaus in *Orestes*.

---

84   The *Odyssey* this time. Penelope's father had the same name as an uncle of Klytemnestra in the Peloponnese, so some people identified the two, and then asked why Telemachus didn't visit his grandfather on his trip to that region in Bk. IV.

85   This is not quite the same as the claim of Agathon quoted at 1456a 24-5 that *many* unlikely things are likely to happen. Aristotle more moderately says that sometimes, when one entertains a charitable reading of a seemingly unaccountable thing, one may find something that accounts for it.

86   Right in the middle of *Medea* the king of Athens happens to cross Medea's path and chats with her for almost a hundred lines. Whatever the scene may contribute to the play, it is given no antecedents or consequences in the story. The *Orestes* is also by Euripides.

So the criticisms people bring are of five forms: that things are either impossible, unaccountable, harmful,[87] contradictory, or contrary to a correctness in accord with an art. And the resolutions of them are to be looked for among the number of kinds mentioned, of which there are twelve.

Chapter 26

One might be at a loss to say whether epic or tragic poetry is the better form of imitation. For if the less crude is the better, and the one directed at a better audience is always of that sort, it is all too clear that the one that imitates everything is crude; for as though the audience could not perceive anything **30** if the actor himself did not add to it, they indulge in a lot of motion, like the low-grade flute players who twist themselves around as though they needed to imitate a discus, and drag the choral leader around when they perform the *Scylla*. Now tragedy is like this, as even the earlier actors believed about those later than themselves, for Mynniskus used to call Callippides an ape for overacting too much, and such used to be the opinion also about **1462a** Pindarus. But the relation these later actors have to those earlier ones, their whole art has toward epic poetry. That art, people say, is for an audience of decent people who have no need to see gestures, while tragedy is for a low sort of people. So if tragedy is crude, it is obvious that it must be worse.

First of all, the accusation is not about the art of the poet but about that of the actors, since it is possible also for the one reciting an epic to overdo it in expressiveness, exactly as Sosistratus used to do, just like Mnasitheus the Opuntian when he was singing in musical contests. Then too, it is not every sort of motion that is to be rejected as unfit, any more than all dancing, but that of low sorts of people; this is the very thing Callipides **10** was blamed for, and now others as well, that they imitate women who are not freeborn. Also, tragedy does what is proper to it even without

---

87   This apparently refers to the complaint about the needless depiction of viciousness.

motion, just as epic poetry does, for it is manifest through reading what particular sort it is. So if it is more powerful in all other respects, it is not necessary for this fault at any rate to belong to it. But then it is more powerful for the reason that it has all the very things that epic poetry does (since it is allowable even for it to use epic's meter), and also no small part of it is the music and the spectacle, by means of which its pleasures are organized most vividly; then too it has this vividness in the reading as well as in the presence of the deeds; also it is more powerful because the end at which the imitation aims **1462b** is present in a shorter length (for what is more concentrated is more pleasant than what is blended into a long time—I mean, for instance, if someone were to put the *Oedipus* of Sophocles into as many lines as the *Iliad*); also, the imitation in epic poetry is less a unity (and a sign of this is that multiple tragedies come out of an epic imitation of any sort whatever, so that if they make one story, it will either appear curtailed if it is exhibited in a short time, or watery if it follows its proper measure of length); I mean, for instance, that if it is put together out of many actions, as the *Iliad* has many such parts and the *Odyssey* as well, and each by each **10** they have magnitude, and yet these poems are organized in the best possible way and are as much as possible imitations each of a single action.

If, then, tragedy is distinguished in all these ways and moreover by the work belonging to the art (for these arts need to produce not any random pleasure but the one described) it is clear that it would be more powerful, since it hits the mark of its end more than epic poetry does.[88]

---

88   It seems that Aristotle regards epic and tragic poetry as sharing an end (wonder), the most important means to it (imitation of an action in a story with reversals, discoveries, and the depiction of suffering), and a characteristic pleasure (the one that comes with the combining of pity and fear). If their work differs, it may have something to do with the cleansing or washing away attributed to tragedy, and the awe-striking power with which it accomplishes its end. These may in turn be related to the intensity produced by its greater concentration. Aristotle credits Homer with bringing his poetry to the highest perfection its form permitted, and the tragedians of later centuries with finding a more effective form.

So about tragedy and epic poetry themselves, and their forms and parts, and how many these are and how they differ, and what the causes are of their being well made or not, and about criticisms and resolutions of them, let this much be said.

Glossary of Names

Poets

Aeschylus (525-456 BC) 1449a; *Libation Bearers* 1455a; *Daughters of Phorcus, Prometheus Bound,* series of plays about Niobe 1456a; *Philoctetes* 1458b; *Mysians* 1460a

Agathon (about 440-401 BC) noted for popularity 1456a; *Antheus* 1451b

Aristophanes (about 450-383 BC) 1448a

Astydamas (4ᵗʰ cent. BC) *Alcmaeon* 1453b

Carcinus (4ᵗʰ cent. BC) noted for obscurity *Thyestes* 1454b; *Amphiarus* 1455a

Chaeremon (4ᵗʰ cent. BC) noted for mixing meters *Centaur* 1447b, 1460a

Chionides (5ᵗʰ cent. BC) writer of comedies 1448a

Cleophon (4ᵗʰ cent. BC) wrote tragedies about ordinary people in flat language 1448a, 1458a

Crates (5ᵗʰ cent. BC) writer of comedies 1449b

Dicaeogenes (5ᵗʰ cent. BC) *Cyprians* 1455a

Empedocles (about 493-433 BC) didactic poet who wrote in hexameters 1447b; *On Nature* 1458a, 1461a; *Purifications* 1457b

Epicharmus (5ᵗʰ cent. BC) writer of comedies 1448a

Euripides (about 485-506 BC) 1453a, 1456a, 1460b; *Iphigeneia Among the Taurians* 1452b, 1454a-b, 1455a-b; *Medea* 1453b, 1454b, 1461b; *Orestes* 1454a, 1461b; *Melanippe the Wise* 1454a; *Iphigeneia at Aulis* 1454a; *Cresphontes* 1454a; series of plays about the sack of Troy 1456a; *Philoctetes* 1458b

Hegemon (4ᵗʰ cent. BC) writer of parodies 1448a

Homer (thought to have lived around 800 BC) 1447b, 1448a-b, 1451a, 1459a-b, 1460a-b; *Iliad* (referred to about a dozen times in Chs. 4, 8, 15, 19, 21, 22, 24, and 26, and a dozen more in Ch. 25); *Odyssey* (more than a dozen references); *Margites* 1448b

Lesches (7th cent. BC) writer of epic poetry *Little Iliad* 1459b

Magnes (5th cent. BC) writer of comedies 1448a

Nicochares (4th cent. BC) writer of parodies *Timidiad* 1448a

Philoxenus (436-380 BC) writer of dithyrambs *Cyclops* 1448a

Sophocles (about 496-406 BC) 1448a, 1449a, 1456a, 1460b; *Oedipus Tyrannus* 1452a, 1453b, 1454b, 1455a, 1460a, 1462b; *Wounded Odysseus* 1453b; *Antigone* 1454a; *Tyro, Tereus* 1454b; *Ajax, Women of Phthia, Peleus* 1455b; *Electra* 1460a

Sophron (about 470-400 BC) and Xenarchus, father and son, writers of dramatic sketches not in meter 1447b

Stasinus (7th cent. BC) writer of epic poetry *Cypria* 1459b

Sthenelus (5th cent. BC) noted for flatness of language 1458a

Theodectes (about 375-334 BC) *Lynceus* 1452a, 1455b; *Tydeus* 1455a

Timotheus (about 450-360 BC) writer of dithyrambs *Cyclops* 1448a; *Scylla* 1454a, 1461b

Works of unknown authorship

Helle 1454a; *Odysseus the False Messenger, Phineidai* 1455a

Titles used by numerous poets

Heracleid, Theseid 1451a

Ajax, Ixion, Peleus, Niobe 1456a

The Judgment of Arms, Philoctetes, Neoptolemus, Euripylus, The Begging, The Laconian Women, The Sack of Troy, The Sailing Home, Sinon, The Trojan Women 1459b

Critics

Ariphrades (probably 5th cent. BC) 1448b

Eucleides (unknown) 1458b

Glaucon (unknown) 1461b

Hippias (unknown) 1461a

Polyidus (unknown) 1455a-b

Xenophanes (about 570-460 BC) 1461a

Painters

Dionysius (5th cent. BC) 1448a

Pauson (probably 5th cent. BC) 1448a

Polygnotus (5th cent. BC) 1448a, 1450a

Zeuxis (5th cent. BC) 1450a, 1461b

Actors, Reciters, Singers

Callipides (4th cent. BC) 1461b, 1462a

Mnaistheus 1462a

Mynniscus (5th cent. BC) 1461b

Pindarus (4th cent. BC) 1461b

Sosistratus 1462a

Glossary of Some Important Greek Words

Alogon, to (something unaccountable) Anything that happens in an imitation of action that is not a necessary or likely result of a choice or a preceding event. This word, and the associated word *alogia*, are never used here for any sort of irrationality within human beings, but only for contrived rescues, unmotivated episodes, and surreal scenes. Aristotle regards thinking as less important than character in giving rise to the action of a tragedy or epic poem (1450b 4), and character involves what is irrational in us just as much as what is rational (*Nicomachean Ethics* 1111b 1-2). 1454b, 1460a, 1461b

Epieikês (decent), *chrêstos* (solidly reliable) Of good character. These are the words Aristotle uses for the central figure in a well-made tragedy, the first referring to the ability to see what action is called for in any circumstances, the second to the stable condition of the soul that makes such action possible. 1452b, 1454a-b, 1462a (See *spoudaios*.)

Êrôikon (heroic) Used here only for verse written in dactylic hexameter. Aristotle never speaks of the central figure in a tragedy or epic as a hero. 1448b, 1459a-b, 1460a

Êthos (state of character) The stable active condition of a soul that makes it fit and apt to choose in certain ways. A state of character consists almost entirely of virtues and vices (1448a 1-4), but not all people have formed characters; Odysseus in the *Odyssey* does (1459b 15), but Neoptolemus in Sophocles' *Philoctetes* is completing the formation of his character before our eyes. This may be the reason Aristotle regards tragedy as possible without depiction of character (1450a 23-26), even though he considers that depiction its second most important component (1450a 38-39). Typically, the action in a tragedy or epic poem follows from a choice which follows from a state of character. 1447a, 1448a-b, 1449b, 1450a-b, 1454a-b, 1459b, 1460a-b

Hamartia (missing the mark) Used primarily for the failure of a good character to achieve a good end, but also for the failure of a poet to achieve an intended effect or of a critic to understand the point of something in a poetic work. Always contained in the word is its fundamental sense of missing one's aim with a spear or arrow. Never anywhere in the word is any reference to a flaw, of character or of any other kind. Associated forms are *hamartanein* and *hamartêma*. 1449a, 1451a, 1453a, 1454b, 1456b, 1460b, 1461b

Katharsis (cleansing) The washing away of something present in pity and fear, that leaves behind an altered kind of pity and fear. The word is applied to tragedy only once and is not explained, but it is replaced by the word *ekplêxis* (awe-striking impact), in which a metaphor of knocking away supersedes that of washing away. What is awe-striking is described as *thaumaston*, a source of wonder. 1449b (Used also at 1455b for the ritual cleansing of a religious statue.)

Logos (speech, a speech) Language in general, talk, or a piece of dialogue. 1447a, 1448a, 1449a-b, 1450a, 1451b, 1454a, 1456a-b (plot) The skeletal framework of a story. 1455a-b (phrase, discourse) A composite sound with meaning, of which some parts have meaning themselves. 1456b, 1457a

Mimêsis (imitation) The presentation to sense-perception of anything in which an intelligent imagination can contemplate aspects of some other thing. (Forms of this word, including *mimeisthai, mimêtikê, mimêma,* and *mimêtês,* are on virtually every page.)

Muthos (story) A coherent presentation of events in a narrative or dramatic imitation, regarded by Aristotle as the soul that holds an epic or tragedy together; *sustasis* (organization) is here used as a synonym for *muthos,* while *logos* is used only for its framework or plot. 1447b, 1450a, 1451a, 1453a, 1454a-b, 1456a, 1459a, and many other places

Philanthropon, to (love of humanity) Used here specifically for the righteous indignation one feels toward undeserved good fortune and the feeling of satisfaction at its loss, though its broader meaning would include pity for anyone who suffers undeserved bad fortune. 1452b 38, 1453a 2, 1456a 21

Poiêsis (poetry) The making of stories or songs in rhythmic language. In other writings, Aristotle uses the word also in a broad sense for the artful making of any product. (Forms of this word, including *poiein, poiêtikê, poiêma,* and *poiêtês,* are on virtually every page.)

Praxis (action) Not any and all human doings, but those deeds that begin with a choice, proceed through an in-between series of necessary or likely consequences, and end with the achieving or failing to achieve an end. 1447a 28, 1449b 36, 1450a 16-25, and frequently throughout

Proairesis (choice) The convergence of deliberate thinking and stable desire in some end foreseen as possible to achieve. Through it, character is revealed. 1450b 9, 1454a 18

Spoudaios (of serious stature) Visibly displaying the highest excellence. In Chs. 2 and 3 Aristotle applies the word to the central figures in old tragedies and epics, but in Ch. 6 he shifts it to the action a tragedy depicts, and in Ch. 9 to the art of poetry itself. 1448a-b, 1449b, 1451b, 1461a (See *epieikês, chrêstos*.)

Sunthesis (composition) The putting together by some external agent of words, actions, or any other sum of parts. 1449 b 35, 1450a 5, 1452b 31, 1458a 28, 1459a 22

Sustasis (organization) The standing together by inherent relations of the parts in a whole. Used here only for the coherence of actions in a story. 1450a 15, 1452a 19, and frequently throughout (It and its corresponding verb *sunistanai* occur about four times as often as *sunthesis* and *suntithesthai*.)

Tragikon (with tragic suffering) Used here specifically for the depiction of suffering, and in the superlative for the depiction of terrible suffering, though it could refer elsewhere to any aspect of or resemblance to tragedy. 1453a 27, 30, b 39, 1456a 21

Tragôdia (tragedy) The imitation in dramatic poetry of an action producing pity and fear. Aristotle regards its form as a gradual evolution out of choral songs such as dithyrambs in honor of Dionysus and its content as already fully developed centuries earlier by the art or natural genius of Homer. (The word is used frequently throughout, with the exception of Chs. 19-21 that deal with aspects of poetry in general, and almost all of 24-25 that deal with epic poetry in particular.)